Christmas - 1980
Maher

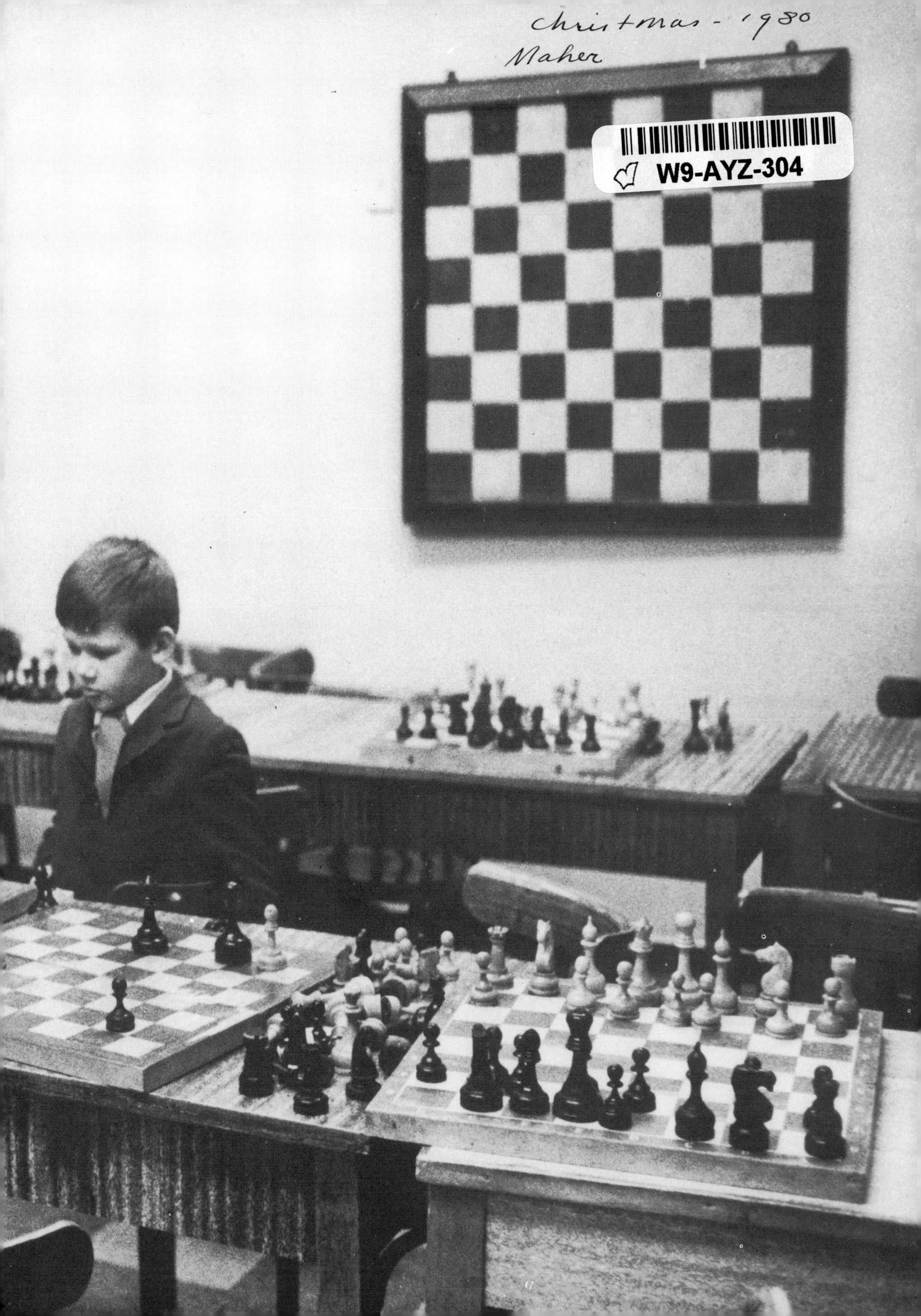

The Children's Book of Chess

US Junior
Joel Benjamin

The Children's Book of Chess

Ted Nottingham
Bob Wade

Crown Publishers, Inc., New York

Acknowledgements

I should like to thank my co-author Bob Wade, whose brilliant scholarship, a by-word in the chess world, has honed this book and given it its fine cutting edge. My grateful thanks are also due to the following: my brother Gordon for all his encouragement; Mrs Phyllis Woodall of Boston for her story 'The Pawn'; Allan R. Lewis, Chairman of the Spalding Chess Club, who gave me the idea of 'The Starship Knight'; my sister-in-law Mrs Jean Nottingham for her typing and Roger Francis for proofreading; and, finally, Alan Hamp of Batsford's for his excellent design and my editor Peter Kemmis Betty for his great interest and encouragement throughout the enterprise.
Ted Nottingham

The Illustrations

Except for the photographs of particular famous young players and those reproduced on pages 2-16, 33 and 36, the illustrations in this book are not intended to relate directly to the text; rather they convey, pictorially, the atmosphere of young players playing chess — with its alternating enjoyment and hard work, excitement and despair, rivalry and companionship.

The Authors and Publishers would like to thank the following for permission to reproduce these photographs:
G. M. Brown for pages 53 and 69; Clive Bubley for pages 2-16, 33 and 36; Camera Press Ltd for pages 28, 31, 40, 42, 45, 61, 75, 88, 95, 101, 102 and 111; *Chess Life and Review* for page 99; Fox Photos Ltd for pages 56 and 107; Burt Hochberg for the frontispiece; Keystone Press Agency Ltd for pages 23, 49, 83 and 91; Alexander Kotov for pages 6, 7 (bottom), 8, 104 and 106, collected from a variety of Soviet sources; Vasily Smyslov for page 7 (top).

The cover illustration, by Clive Bubley, was taken at Kitwood Girls School, Lincolnshire and shows a group of young players from South Lincolnshire schools watching a five-minute game between Robert Seaman and Sally Atkin.

© Ted Nottingham and R.G. Wade
First published in USA by Crown Publishers, Inc., 1979
Printed in Great Britain

Library of Congress Cataloging in Publication Data

Nottingham, Ted.
    The children's book of chess.

    SUMMARY: Discusses the pieces, moves, rules, and strategy of chess and youthful champions of the game.
    1. Chess--Juvenile literature. [1. Chess.
2. Games]   I. Wade, Bob, 1920- joint author.
II. Title.
GV1446.N67   794.1'2   78-19121
ISBN 0-517-53578-5

Contents

The Great Learn Young

You're never too old to begin playing chess. You're never too young either.

Paul Morphy learnt to play at 10 from his father and uncle. When he was 12, he twice beat a famous Hungarian player visiting his home town, New Orleans. In 1858, when 21, Paul visited Europe and convincingly beat the best players in the world.

See this list of world champions:

Wilhelm Steinitz learnt at 12. He reigned as leading player from 1866 to 1894.

Emanuel Lasker (champion 1894-1921), when 10, was taught by his older brother, Berthold.

José Raoul Capablanca was the best 4-year-old chessplayer of all time. He quietly picked up the moves by watching his father playing with a friend. One day his father moved a knight not according to the rules — it went from one white square to another white one — and won. Then

The young Capablanca

young José showed his secret knowledge by pointing out the error. Embarrassed, his father challenged the boy to a game — and lost! A few days later he took his son to the local chess club. At 12 Capablanca was champion of Cuba and he was world champion from 1921 to 1927.

Alexander Alekhine (champion 1927-35, 1937-45) was not yet 12 when he started. As a boy he played many games by post.

Max Euwe (champion 1935-37) was taught by his mother when he was 4. He won his first tournament at 10.

Mikhail Botvinnik (champion 1948-57, 1958-60, 1961-63) learnt and played in his first tournament at 12. Next year he won his school championship.

Vasily Smyslov with his father

Vasily Smyslov (champion 1957-58) had, by the time he was 6½, an intelligent knowledge of the moves.

Bobby Fischer

Tigran Petrosian (champion 1963-69) was not yet 9 when he learnt the moves by watching play at the officers' club where his father was a caretaker.

Bobby Fischer's sister taught him when he was 6. He became champion of the United States when he was 14 and a grandmaster at 15. He won the world title in 1972, but gave it up without play in 1975.

Mikhail Tal's father was a doctor and had a chess set in his waiting room. Tal watched the patients playing. By the age of 10 he had won at school a diploma for chess. He was champion in 1960-61.

Boris Spassky (champion 1969-72) learnt when he was 5, as an evacuee from the besieged city of Leningrad.

Anatoly Karpov (champion 1975-) learnt at 4. Although he lived in a mountainous part of Russia, he made steady progress: he was a third category player at 7, second at 9, first at 9, candidate master at 11, USSR master at 15, International Master at 18, International Grandmaster at 19 and World Champion at 23.

And the women champions:

Vera Menchik, first women's world champion (from 1927 until she was killed in 1944), learnt at 9, but only really became strong at 17, when she came to live at Hastings in England.

Nona Gaprindashvili (champion since 1962) learnt at 5. She made a habit of winning family tournaments against her five brothers.

The Battleground

Chess is fought on an 8 x 8 board. This must be placed between the players in such a way that the **right** hand corner square nearest each is a **white** one.

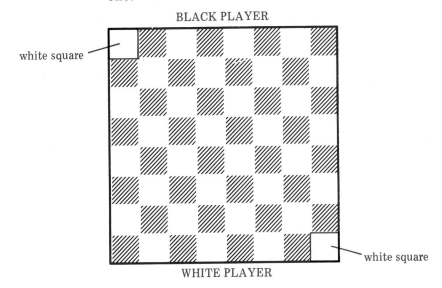

BLACK PLAYER

white square

white square

WHITE PLAYER

Each square can be named. We use the simplest system — the algebraic. It is based on the first eight letters of the alphabet a,b,c,d,e,f,g, and h and the numbers 1 to 8.

The right hand corner square nearest the white player is h1 — the junction of the h-file and rank-1. Nearest to black is a8. Try naming some squares. d4 is where the d-file and rank-4 meet.

By custom the white chessmen are always set up along ranks 1 and 2 and the black along 7 and 8.

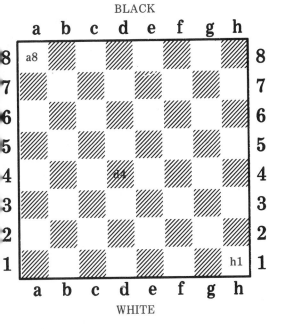

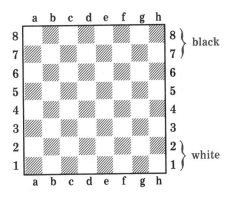

The Pawn Game

In South Lincolnshire, England, we start off chess with the pawn game, in which the winner is the first to push a pawn through to the far rank.

The pawns have very simple moves. See how they go from the following photos and diagrams of a sample game.

This is the starting position for the pawn game. White will begin.

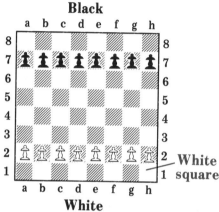

The white pawns are lined up along the second rank. Your opponent's black pawns are along the seventh.

When we begin a full game the empty squares behind the pawns will be occupied by pieces.

1 c2 — c4

As you see, your white 'c'-pawn is being moved two squares forward.

All pawns can move two squares forward on their first move.

If you wish you need only move them **one** square forward.

1...   d7 — d6

Your opponent has moved a pawn only one square.

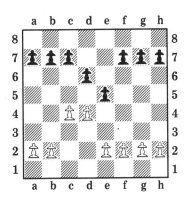

In the diagram the black 'e'-pawn is one square diagonally forward from your 'd'-pawn. Your 'd'-pawn can take his 'e'-pawn.

2 d2 — d4
You boldly push a neighbouring pawn two squares.

2...   e7 — e5
He is moving one of his pawns two squares forward.

3 d4xe5
Your 'd'-pawn is capturing his 'e'-pawn. 'x' means takes.
A pawn takes diagonally one square forward.
When capturing, you are taking off his black pawn and putting your white one **in its place.**

3...   d6xe5
His 'd'-pawn is capturing your
pawn on the e-file.

4...   f7 — f5
He moves his 'f'-pawn two.
    Pawns only go forward. They
move straight forward. They
take diagonally one square
forward.

4 b2 — b4
You move your 'b'-pawn two.

5 a2 — a4
You move your 'a'-pawn two.

5...   e5 — e4

He is moving his 'e'-pawn again, but now it can only go one square. **After its first go each pawn can be played only one square per move.**

6 c4 — c5

Your 'c'-pawn is marching on.

   Remember. The player whose pawn first reaches the far side of the board wins the game.

6...   f5 — f4

His 'f'-pawn moves forward.

7 b4 — b5

Your 'b'-pawn goes on.

7...   g7 — g5

He's advanced his 'g'-pawn two squares.

8 a4 — a5

Your 'a'-pawn is pushed on. The big clash is just ahead.

8...   e4—e3
His 'e'-pawn has moved again. It
could take one of your pawns.

9 f2xe3
You take first with your 'f'-pawn.

9...   f4xe3
He's recapturing with his 'f'-pawn.
The new 'e'-pawns block each
other and cannot move.

You think.
    The first pawn home wins. But
how can any of your three advanced
pawns find a way past his three?

10 b5—b6
You thrust your central 'b'-pawn
forward. You would like to take
either his 'a' or 'c'-pawn. They also
can take.

10...   c7xb6
He's chosen to take with his 'c'-
pawn.

You think hard.

Your 'c'-pawn could be played straight ahead. It has only three squares to go. Careful! If you immediately advance it, his b7-pawn gobbles it. Wish that black pawn was somewhere else.

12 c5 — c6
Your wish is granted. His b7-pawn has gone.

Now your 'c'-pawn has a clear path. Advance!

11 a5 — a6
You confidently advance your 'a'-pawn. It is two squares — b7 and b8 — away from victory.

12...   b5
He rushes forward his passed 'b'-pawn. But it will not be quick enough.

11...   b7xa6
He takes it. He must.

13 c6 — c7
Your 'c'-pawn reaches the 7th rank.

13...   b5 — b4
His 'b'-pawn moves again.

14 c7 — c8
You push your 'c'-pawn home.
You've won.

In a normal game of chess, using all the pieces, this pawn is now exchanged for a white queen.

These pawns block each other and cannot move.

Which black pawns can capture? How do the black pawns take?

Either this way, or

that.

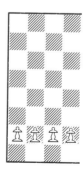

How do the white pawns begin?

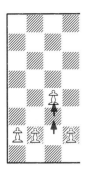

Either two squares ahead — like this, or

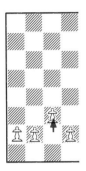

one square — thus.
But after a pawn has been moved, its right to move two squares is lost.

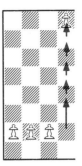

What happens to every pawn reaching the far rank?

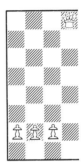

It is replaced as part of the same move, by a queen — as here — or, in a most exceptional case, by another piece.
Note that a side can have more than one queen.

'The Pawn'

The pawn stood on the board with the rest of the set. This was his first game and he was afraid. He had dwelt with his fellow chessmen in the box for a long time.

It had been safe and comfortable. But now he felt he had to prove himself. Standing there black and shiny, he felt his fear disappear and a powerful feeling take its place. He was going to make a brilliant move. He was going to be the most important piece on the board. With bold assurance he moved.

There was a gasp of shock around him. He had made a mistake. A firm hand picked him up and threw him back in the box. He lay there shivering with disgust at his stupidity.

He didn't want to face anyone. He wanted to hide forever.

After a time he was placed on the board again. This time he was cautious, less afraid. Thinking hard, he moved. He gained confidence and checked.

Then to his dismay he was put unceremoniously back in the box. He lay still, the pain of his failure filling him.

A knight spoke to him.

'Do you really think you have any power in these games?' he said. 'Don't be such a conceited fool. You're nothing unless someone moves you intelligently. And that would be difficult with the children here. They think they're playing tiddlywinks.'

The knight sighed in a resigned manner. 'It's being with all these sad resigned people,' he yawned and dozed off — rather like the Dormouse in *Alice in Wonderland*. The pawn was subdued. He had lost everything and nothing mattered any more.

And then it happened. This thing that gave him back his value to himself. He was standing once more on the front row. A little less black, a little less shiny.

A hand moved him here and there. Like a simple country dance. He was so certain. He was so sure of the right move. He seemed to push this idea into the player's mind.

The hand hesitated. The pawn became an ache of force to make his player move the right way.

The player concentrated. As if receiving a message, the hand nodded. The pawn was moved. And to the delight of the pawn and player, he became a queen and the game was won. The pawn had found an excitement that would be there forever — in taking part in a well-fought game of chess.

'Pawns are the soul of chess', said the great player André Philidor.

The Queen

In modern chess she is the fastest thing on the board. This was not always so, for back in the middle ages she could only move one square diagonally at a time.

The French of the thirteenth century called this new queen the 'mad queen'.

She can move in any straight line, up, down, along, diagonally, back and forth. As far as she likes. But no jumping! To take she lands on a piece.

She is worth almost twice as much as any other piece on the board, except the king. World champion Capablanca once wanted to introduce a new piece he called an 'Ambassador' which could move like a queen and jump like a knight. But his idea did not become a hit. Chess's queen is powerful enough. Like a starship against aeroplanes.

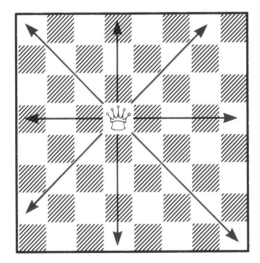

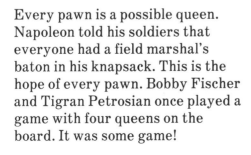

Every pawn is a possible queen. Napoleon told his soldiers that everyone had a field marshal's baton in his knapsack. This is the hope of every pawn. Bobby Fischer and Tigran Petrosian once played a game with four queens on the board. It was some game!

Fischer has the white pieces. Only 16 at the time, he was playing one of the greatest grandmasters of the age. In fact Tigran — 'The Tiger' — Petrosian was in a few years to be world champion himself. But remember, one extra queen is usually enough to build a mating net.

Can you handle the Mad Queen?

Queen v pawns: special game
Rule: If one pawn gets through to the far row, its side wins.

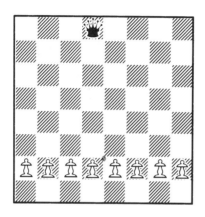

It's lonely, but you will soon see the power of this queen as it blasts through the poorly protected pawns.

The queen always starts on the square of their own colour. Black queen on a black square. White queen on a white. So the black queen stands on d8; the white queen would start on d1.

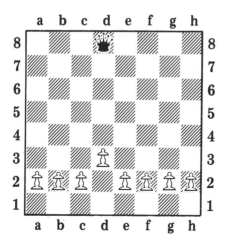

1 d2 — d3

White moves first and rescues this pawn. The queen should not now take the pawn on d3 because it is protected by the pawns on c2 and e2.

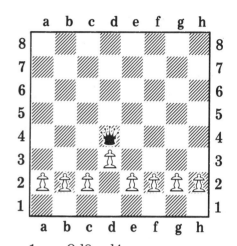

1...   Qd8 — d4

The queen leaps into battle and strikes two ways — at the pawns on b2 and f2.

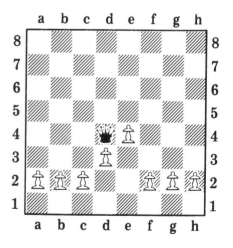

2 e2 — e4

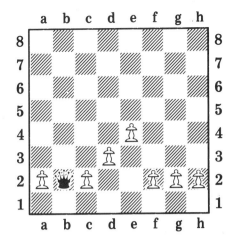

2...   Qd4xb2

The queen decides on the pawn at b2.

Have you got used yet to the letters underneath the diagram?

White looks to see whether he can push his advanced 'e'-pawn further. No! The black queen could take it.

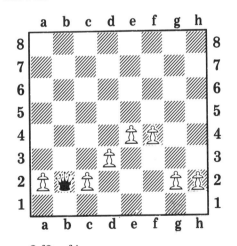

3 f2 — f4

White plays his 'f'-pawn two squares.

The queen now has the choice of two pawns.

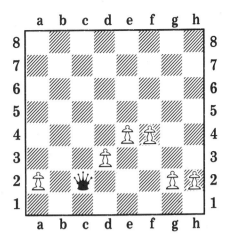

3...   Qb2xc2

Do you notice the capture sign 'x' again?

The queen captures to get rid of the dangerous pawns in the middle.

How many pawns are now attacked?

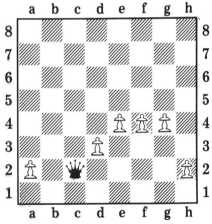

4 g2 — g4

Another pawn races forward.

Three of them are only four squares away!

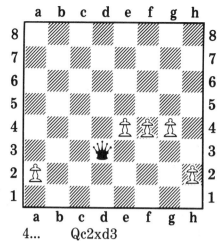

4...   Qc2xd3

The queen captures on d3 and
chases the advanced group.

    Three gone, five left.

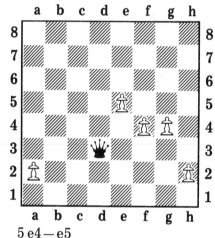

5 e4 — e5

Get away from the queen!

    Three squares to victory.

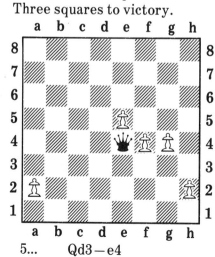

5...   Qd3 — e4

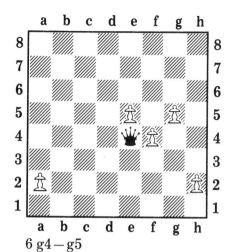

6 g4 — g5

Two pawns are now only three
squares away.

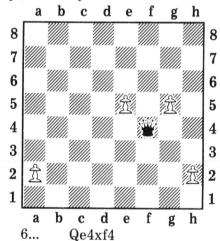

6...   Qe4xf4

Another 'x' sign. Take.

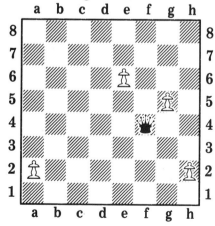

7 e5 — e6

Two away!

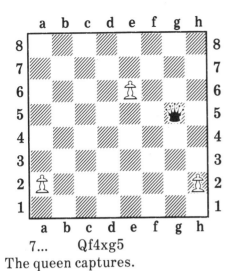

7...   Qf4xg5

The queen captures.

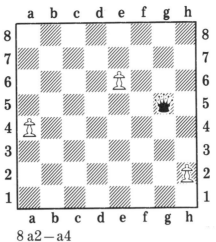

8 a2 — a4

Too late. Now the queen has only to mop up.

The last game

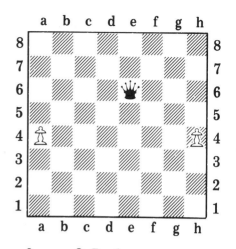

8...   Qg5—e7

9...   Qe7xe6

Two left.

The black queen has two plans.

The queen can now wait on squares along the third rank such as c6, d6, e6 and f6 until the pawns arrive on a6 and h6 to be taken. Or the queen can be played to a6, take the 'a'-pawn, and then go to the 'h'-file and remove the last pawn.

The queen has won. But try using it alone when you are having a game with all the pieces and serious players will laugh at you. It's a striker working best with full support from other pieces.

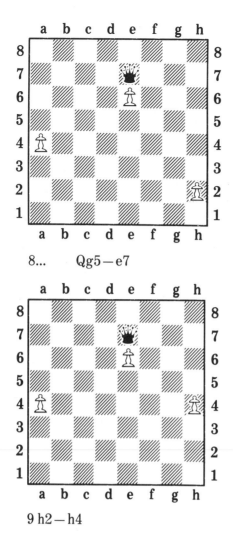

9 h2—h4

Your turn now

Try it with you having the queen and your opponent the pawns; and then change over and try again.

Another idea:
queen and pawns v queen and pawns

Queens start on squares of their own colour. Black queen at d8 and white at d1.

Try with queen and 8 pawns each to be first to 'queen' a pawn.

Try these sort of games as often as you can. When you know how the king, knight, bishop and rook move, try each of them with your pawn team.

Master each piece. Then handling an army comes much easier.

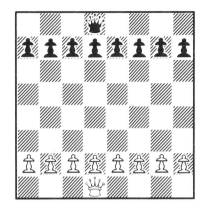

Pinned

Can you see why your white pawn cannot afford to take the black pawn?

Or again here. Why should your pawn not take the black one?

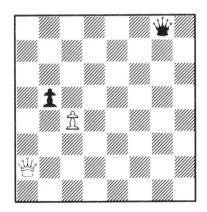

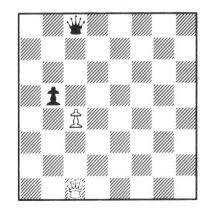

If you get the answers to these two, you have done well. It saves you from losing your queen.

In both examples the white pawn at c4 is 'pinned'. Watch for such pins in your games.

The King

Some idea of the value of the king can be gained from these modern ratings of the pieces.

Rook	Knight	Bishop	King	Queen	Pawn
.	.	.	.	.	.
5	3	3	100	9 or 10	1

Your king is the most important piece, worth far more than all your other pieces. Even the 100 rating may be misleading for its value. True is infinity — a number that cannot be counted. It is the 'jackpot' piece. If your king is caught you lose the game.

If the king is attacked by an enemy piece we say it is in 'check'.

Though the king is important its move is very limited. It can be moved in any direction — forward, backward, along, diagonally — only **one square.**

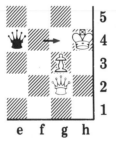

The king is 'checked'.
On the very next move **the check must be stopped by**
(1) moving the king off the line of attack, in this case to h3, h5 or g5

or
(2) putting a chessman between the king and the attacking piece.

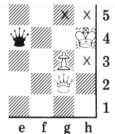

Pawn has moved forward and blocked the check.

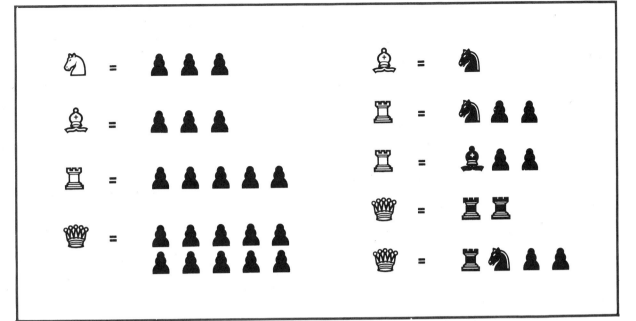

or
(3) capturing the attacker.

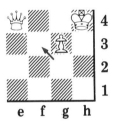

The white queen has captured the checking queen.

The king can never be put on a square which is covered by an opponent's piece, or even by an opponent's king.

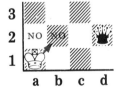

The king cannot move to the two NO squares because the queen covers them.

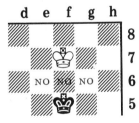

Neither king can move to the three squares marked NO. They are contested by the opposing king. They are no-kings' land.

If by oversight the king is left on, or is played onto, a square on which it is attacked, the position must be put back to the one before the oversight, and a legal move played.

Royal Duel

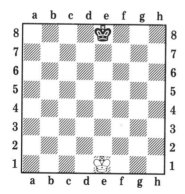

The starting position for the two kings is at the ends of the 'e'-line, white king e1, black e8.

Idea of this game: in the duel between the kings, the first through to the other side of the board wins. Remember the king moves only one square at a time but in any direction.

White always starts first.

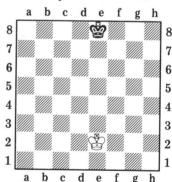

1 Ke1 — e2

My king should then get to the other end first, unless your king blocks me.

Now I am only six squares away. You are seven. So, if you are going to have any hope with the black king, you must block mine.

1...   Ke8—e7

Six each now. But you are Black and
it would be foolish to try and outrun
my white king.

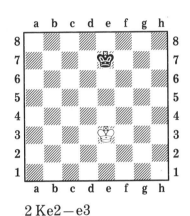

2 Ke2—e3

Five to go now!

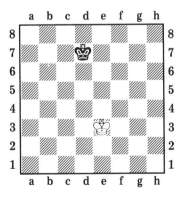

2...   Ke7—d7

You give up trying to race and plan
to block my king.

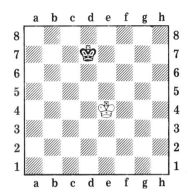

3 Ke3—e4

My king continues his march.

Only four moves now to the other
side.

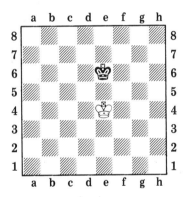

3...   Kd7—e6

A very good move.

Remember, the king is so
important that it is not allowed to
be put where it can be taken. The
white king is not permitted to go
next to the black one. The way
forward is blocked.

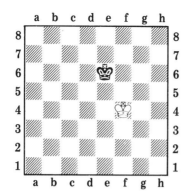

4 Ke4 — f4

Still four squares away.

But your black king is five squares away and so there is no point in trying to race.

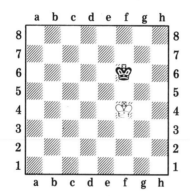

4...   Ke6 — f6

Again your king blocks the way.

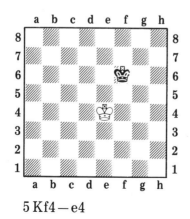

5 Kf4 — e4

Because the way forward is blocked, the white king is forced sideways.

What will you do as Black now?

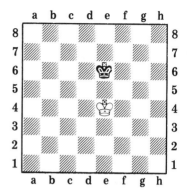

5...   Kf6 — e6

Rightly Black continues to block. Maybe White will retreat.

Now go back to after Black's second (Ke1 — e2 Ke8 — e7 2 Ke2 — e3 Ke7 — d7) and see if you can win by 3 Ke3 — f4. You should.

Put the kings again at e1 and e8. After practice you should find that when White starts, White always wins. It's not a fair duel!

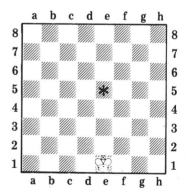

Royal Choice

Can you see how many ways it will be possible to take the white king at e1 to e5 in only four moves? The simplest is Ke1 — e2 — e3 — e4 — e5; another is Ke1 — d2 — c3 — d4 — e5.

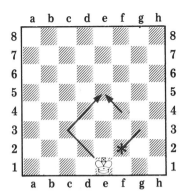

How many ways? There are 43.

Now please try this game: the kings with their pawn teams.

Remembering that queens stand on squares of their own colour, it is easy to fix the position of the king.

The same rule: first pawn safely through to the other side wins.

The best plan in this game is to move a centre pawn quickly and get the king up the board as quickly as possible to capture enemy pawns. A great world champion, Steinitz, once said 'the king is a powerful piece'. Use it in this game and see. But beware! Use him in the open only after the dangerous teams of pieces have been swapped off.

Outdoor chess in the Soviet Union

Checkmate

When the king is attacked on the square where it stands, and there is no way of:

1 capturing the attacker, or

2 putting a chessman in the way, or

3 moving it to a safe square,

then it is checkmate.

It is, naturally, polite to tell your opponent you have attacked his king by saying 'check'.

Our word 'checkmate' is really the Persian words 'shah mat' which means: 'the king is dead'. 'Shah mat' was passed by word of mouth through many countries and many hundreds of years until in English it became checkmate. Surround and attack the king — this is the ultimate purpose.

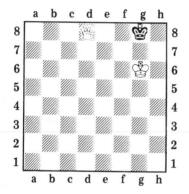

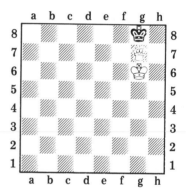

This is checkmate!

The queen attacks the king.

He cannot step sideways to f8 or h8. The queen also attacks these squares.

The king cannot step forward on to squares covered by the other king. This is not allowed.

It's checkmate.

This is also checkmate.

The black king cannot move to f8 or h8 because of the white queen. He cannot go to f7 h7 or g7 and take the queen, because those squares are covered by the white king. This is not allowed. So, this too is checkmate.

The fifty-move rule.

When you only have a king left, you draw if your opponent fails to checkmate you in 50 of his moves. Except that every time something is taken or a pawn moved, you must go back to 0 and start counting again.

King and Queen v King

The ending king and queen versus king is very important. It often happens that someone has an extra pawn and promotes it into a queen. It is very frustrating to be a queen up and not know how to win.

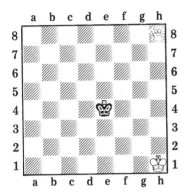

The pawn has just reached the other side and become a queen. The 50-move rule starts now.

You should not need 50; it should take much less. If you practise this hard you can get it down to about 10 moves. I'm going to show you a checkmate from one of the hardest positions of king and queen against a lone king.

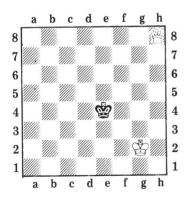

1 Kh1 — g2
By itself the queen cannot give mate on the open board. The king must help.

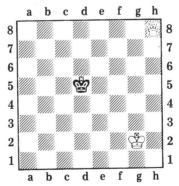

1... Ke4 — d5
The black king wants to stay in the centre as long as possible. It can only be checkmated on the edge of the board — so it stays in the centre.

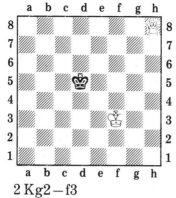

2 Kg2—f3

The white king is needed so it continues to head for the action!

Steinitz said, 'The king is a strong piece'. The checkmate comes remarkably quickly if the king is used.

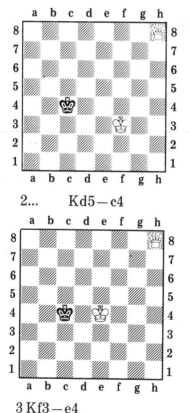

2... Kd5—c4

3 Kf3—e4

The white king continues his march against the black king.

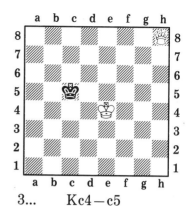

3... Kc4—c5

Gradually the black king is pushed back to the edge of the board.

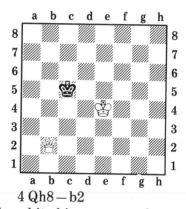

4 Qh8—b2

The white king cannot advance; so in comes the queen to cut off more of the black king's ground.

Remember, the king cannot move onto squares covered by enemy pieces, or even by the enemy king. This would be moving into check.

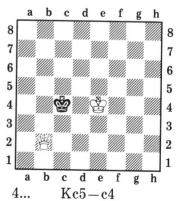

4... Kc5—c4

Now the two kings are facing each

other and the black king cannot move on to squares beside the white king.

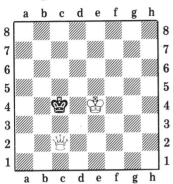

5 Qb2—c2 check

The king is checked and because of the queen's power cannot move onto any square along the 'c'-line. He cannot also move towards the white king.

So. . .back he goes.

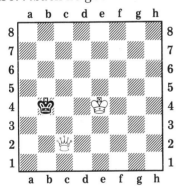

5...   Kc4—b4

The black king has now only the 'b'-line and the 'a'-line left to him.

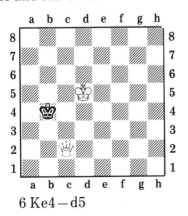

6 Ke4—d5

The king moves forward again.

6...   Kb4—b5

And now the black king's path to the 'c'-line is totally blocked by the white king's command of the squares c4, c5 and c6.

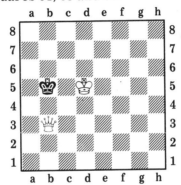

7 Qc2—b3 check

The queen gives check knowing the king can only step back onto the 'a'-line.

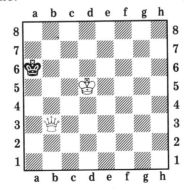

7...   Kb5—a6

The king is driven to the edge of the board. Here checkmate can be given.

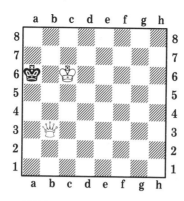

8 Kd5 — c6

The white king bores in, blocking the approaches to the 'b'-line, which are cut off by the queen as well.

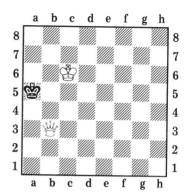

8... Ka6 — a5

There is no way out now.

9 Qb3 — b5 mate

Qb3 — a3 would also have been mate. If the black king had gone to a7, then the queen would mate on b7.

Every square the king can move to is covered by the white queen or king. It cannot take the queen which protected by the white king.

Beware of stalemate

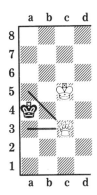

The white king and queen command all the squares around the black king. But it is not checkmate. It's not even check. It's completely against rules for the black king to move to any neighbouring square. His side has no other piece or pawn move. It is stalemate. He is stalled. The game is now drawn.

Here is another stalemate. The white queen controls all the king's escape squares.

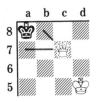

Beware! Do not move the white king to c6, c7 or c8 as the black king

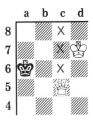

would be stalemated. And other people will think that you are stupid. Instead, play your queen to b4, then next move bring the white king to c6 and...

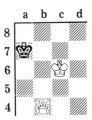

give mate on the following move; 1 Qc5 — b4 Ka6 — a7 2 Kd7 — c6 Ka7-a8 3 Qb4 — b7 checkmate. If, on move 2, the black king had been played to a6. White has three different queen moves to give checkmate — at a3, a4 and b6.

The Knight

In olden times he was the horseman. In Germany he is called 'springer', which means jumper. He has been described as the invisible piece. This is because he has such a funny move. His move is best described as 'L'-shaped.

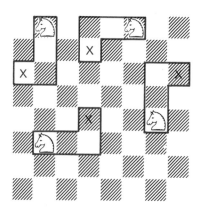

He can go to the squares marked X.

Two squares up, down or along, then turn right or left and go one more square. 'L'-shape.

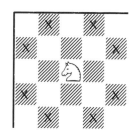

He is the only piece that can jump over other men.

Also he only takes from the square on which he ends his move.

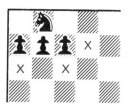

Exercising the Knight

The white knight has to take all the black pawns which are fixed and do not move.

How many moves will it take you? Try.

This way's my way.

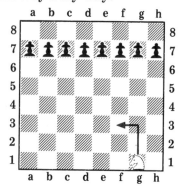

1 Ng1 — f3

White plays his knight from g1 to f3.

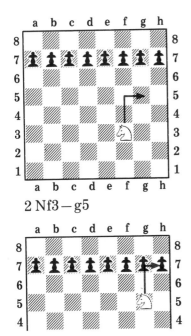

2 Nf3 — g5

3 Ng5xh7

White plays knight on g5 takes whatever is on h7 — a black pawn;

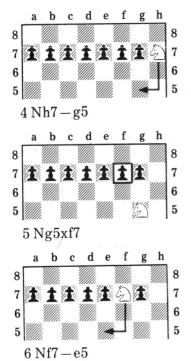

4 Nh7 — g5

5 Ng5xf7

6 Nf7 — e5

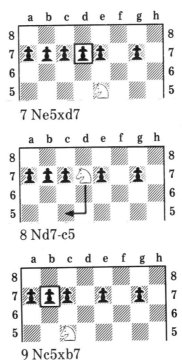

7 Ne5xd7

8 Nd7-c5

9 Nc5xb7

Next comes a tricky three-step turn:

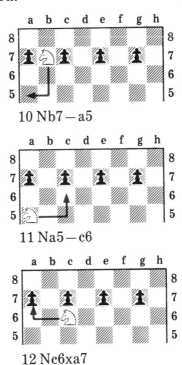

10 Nb7 — a5

11 Na5 — c6

12 Nc6xa7

From the next diagram White plays the knight first to b5, second takes c7, third goes to d5, fourth takes e7, fifth goes to f5, and last takes g7 — six moves.

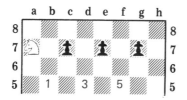

Total: 18 moves.

This is not the only way to do this in 18 moves. But you cannot do it in less.

Can you do it and also find other ways?

Watching: Leonard Barden and David, Nigel Short's father

Playing: Nigel Short and Vasily Smyslov

The Starship Knight

James McMahon, the very young captain of the W.S.S. *Armstrong*, was in trouble. On his first star tour, he had been travelling in a remote part of the Milky Way. Now here he was on Procyon 5 with his crew of sixteen, which included his young wife, Matilda, a prisoner of the Cyonites.

His blurred senses gradually took in the situation within the trial room. One Cyonite in particular drew his attention. The creature, except for a ruff growing around his neck, looked like a human. It was talking with the aid of a standard Milky Way translator pack on its shoulder.

McMahon's thoughts clicked. The Cyonite was offering one chance. A single combat duel between him and the Cyonite leader. If McMahon won, the prisoners would be freed. If not...

Lights flashed. The green lighting of the room dimmed, and, across the width of one wall, like on a cinema screen, appeared a gigantic chessboard. Only sixteen white pieces showed. McMahon understood. They represented his crew. Each capture would mean death for one of them. He looked around for Matilda and saw her tense face.

In place of the black pieces the Cyonite was to have only a mystery piece. This piece would move in a definite pattern, but it would always remain invisible. The Cyonite and he moved to a gleaming control panel. James swallowed hard. His tongue felt very dry. He did not want to lose any of his crew. He decided on caution. He pressed a button and a pawn moved one forward on the giant screen. Lights flashed as his opponent answered immediately.

The white position took shape. Beads of sweat glimmered on McMahon's forehead. The brain of a man contains more cells than there are stars in the universe — it seemed as if he was using them all. His mind raced through his star ship's library.

A yellow light bathed the screen. A pawn on the king's side disappeared. Guards moved towards the crew and took the ship's engineer to a black circle in the centre of the room. There he was dissolved into nothing.

James McMahon trembled. He gripped the control panel hard and brought his concentration back onto the position. In that room thinking was not easy, but something was nagging at the back of his mind. He felt that the answer to the flashing lights — the mystery piece that was touring the board — was very near. Suddenly, he knew. He did not know how he knew, but he knew!

First, he made sure that there were no further captures of his crew. One of his pieces was 'threatened'. He moved it away. The lights flashed again. Now James McMahon knew exactly where the mystery piece was. He slanted his bishop across the board. Next move he pounced with it. The room lights came on again and the giant chessboard was no more. McMahon blinked. Then there was long dark hair in his face. He gave his wife a long, long kiss. The voice sounded and said 'Take them to their vessel'.

As Procyon 5 faded away and became just one star amidst many, James McMahon explained his victory. He ordered a book to be brought from the library. It was old and the pages had yellowed. It was H. J. R. Murray's great *History of Chess* written back in the twentieth century. In it was described the 'Knight's Tour'. How the knight went to every square of the chessboard without covering any square more than once. Impishly he looked at Matilda. Laughter greeted his next remark: 'You were next.'

The Knight's Tour

Try the knight's tour. It's to go to every square once only. As the knight lands marks the square with an odd chessman, counter, piece of cardboard. You'll need some method.

This was my system. In my mind I divided the board in two areas: (1) the outer two frames (the two edge rows all the way around) and (2) the inner 4 x 4 sanctum. I planned to cover all the outer frames first.

outer frames

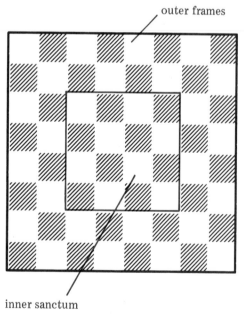

inner sanctum

From a1 I went round the board the same way as the hands go round the clock for 24 moves. Then only inner c3 was available.

Hopefully I continued clockwise around the frame via a4 reaching square b2 on move 37. I was faced with a choice between two inner squares d3 and c4. I thought of the Cyonite. I selected d3 and went clockwise via c1 round the outer frames until I had filled them all in by move 50. Fourteen inner squares to go. I thought. It's going to be a tight fit. I experimented. I unwound. I went anti-clockwise! The last squares were completed.

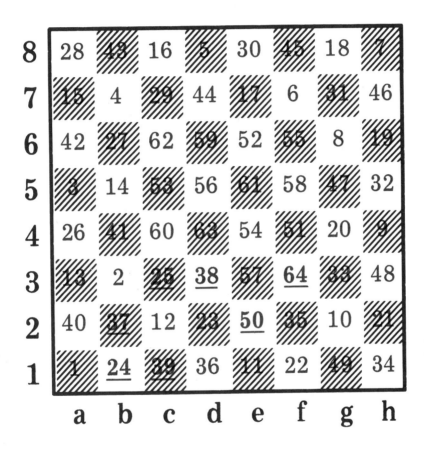

The Bishop

You have two bishops:
One stands on black squares,
Moves on diagonal black squares,
Never moves on white squares.

The other stands on white squares,
Never moves on black squares,
Never crosses black squares,
Moves on diagonal white squares.

They never meet.

Put one in the corner;
He's sleepy.
Put one at the side;
He's lazy.
Put one in the centre;
How strong he is!

Bishops want diagonals open.
Don't hide them in the church,
Don't block their paths with pawns;
You know they cannot jump.

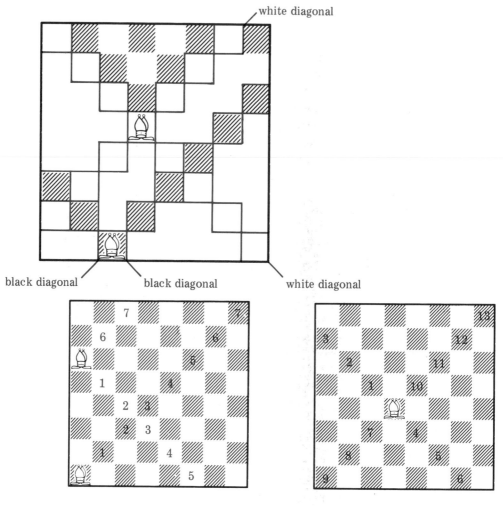

white diagonal

black diagonal   black diagonal   white diagonal

Only 7 squares at most.   Perhaps 13 squares!

Diagonal Exercises

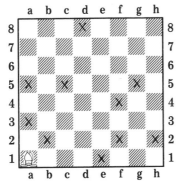

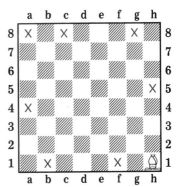

Put a coin or other marker on each square (a3, a5, b2, c5, d8, e1, f2, f4, g5 and h2) marked X.

Move the bishop so as each move to land on a marked square. That's how they capture.

Bishops go along only one diagonal per move.

If on any move you fail, start again.

Answer: Ba1 — b2 — a3 — c5 — f2 — e1 — a5 — d8 — g5 — f4 — h2

Place seven markers on the white diagonals in such a way that there is one marker on each diagonal.

Sample answer: a4, a8, b1, c8, f1, g8 and h5.

Light and dark squares help one to see straight along diagonals.

Bishops move straight along diagonals. They don't jump. They'll take anything but a king on their landing square.

Question: How many moves is needed for one bishop to capture each marker? 9? 11? 13?

Bishop v Knight

'Which is better: the bishop or the knight?' is one of the great arguments of chess. While everybody agrees the queen is the strongest and, after her, the rook (whose power you will see soon), people disagree about the bishop and the knight. With the diagonals clear the bishop is strong. The knight can jump where everything else is blocked.

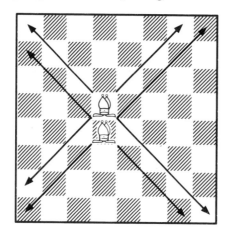

Keeping the bishop pair is commonly preferred. As the game goes on the board clears.

But make up your own mind according to the particular position.

Have a look at some of these.

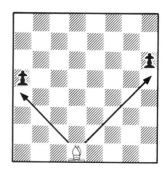

These two black pawns are ready to advance. They are on opposite sides of the board, yet still they cannot get past the bishop, whose power along the diagonals stops both of them. The knight with his shorter move could not possibly do this.

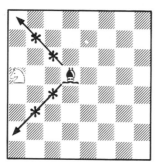

The bishop has trapped the knight at the side of the board. All its escape squares are covered by the bishop. While the bishop can do this, there is nothing similar for the knight.

This is when the bishop is weak. The bishop stands on a white diagonal but is blocked by his own pawns. If the pawns get blocked on the white squares the knight will be much more dangerous.

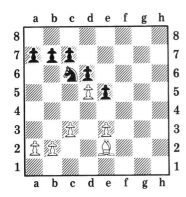

A move to the side of the board is generally not as good as one to the centre. Why? Because the knight can only go one way at the side. He cannot jump off the board. Also here all available further squares are guarded by either the white 'a'-pawn or the bishop.

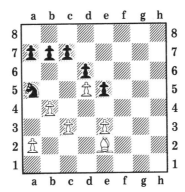

The pawn on b2 goes to b4 and the knight is trapped.

Have another look at the top diagram and suggest another move for the knight rather than to the side of the board.

...Nc6 — e7

Be careful of this

The white pawn has just moved to d5.

The knight is attacked by it and has to move.

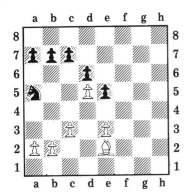

Noah's Ark Trap

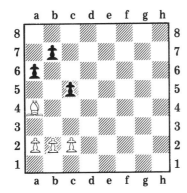

We have seen the knight trapped at the side of the board, so it is only fair to show a bishop hemmed in and trapped. So many people for so long have been caught by the following manoeuvre that it is called the 'Noah's Ark Trap'. The black 'b'-pawn moves to b5.

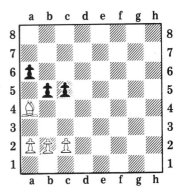

The bishop moves back to b3.

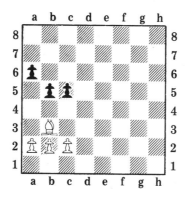

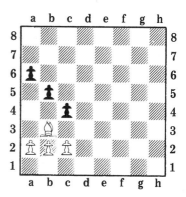

The bishop is now in front of its pawns at b3.

Can you see how it is going to be trapped?

The black 'c'-pawn has come to c4.

The white bishop is now trapped.

At the side of the board it is very easy to get both the knight and the bishop trapped.

Place the Knight well

Let us see where the knight is placed best.

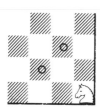

In the corner of the board the knight only covers 2 squares.

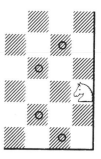

Two squares along from the corner and the knight covers 4 squares.

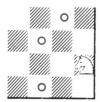

One square in from the corner, the knight still only covers 3 squares.

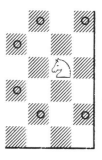

One file in from the side of the board and now well away from the corner, the knight covers 6 squares.

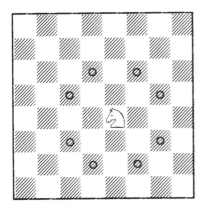

In the centre of the board the knight covers 8 squares. When you are playing chess, ask yourself all the time, 'where is my knight best placed?' The exact best can depend on other pieces.

Some Knight Forks

The knight attacks both the king and the queen.

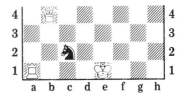

A 'family' fork! The black knight forks king, queen and rook.

Jonathan Penrose, *left*, born in 1933, was champion of London at the age of 15, a feat which no one else in this country has ever matched. In 1960 be beat the Russian world champion Mikhail Tal in a marvellous game. Penrose is one of England's greats. Let us have a look at a game where he shows us how to attack with knight forks. It was played in the 1950 British championship.

49

Penrose is Black and it is his move.

Just watch the damage done by his knight, now on f6.

1...   Bc5xf2 check

Penrose's bishop darts in to take a pawn, and also gives check to the white king.

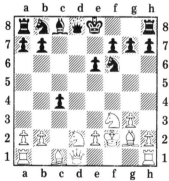

Walter Veitch, an experienced player, must have wondered at the young Penrose's move.

He takes the bishop.

2 Ke1xf2

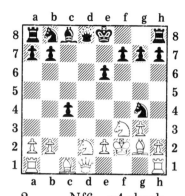

2...   Nf6 — g4 check

The black knight comes in to do its damage.

Now let us have a look at the possible moves before we look at the one Walter Veitch chose.

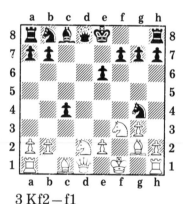

3 Kf2 — f1

If Veitch had played this he would have been in for a nasty shock. **Then**

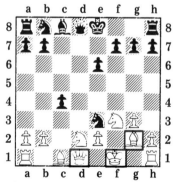

3...   Ng4 — e3 check

The black knight forks the king, queen and bishop.

This is why Veitch did not play
Kf2—f1.
If

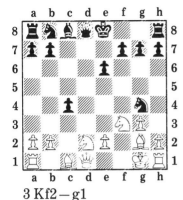

3 Kf2—g1

then mate follows by

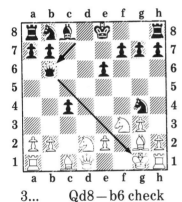

3...   Qd8—b6 check

and after the king moves to f1 (or
the pawn blocks by going to e3, the
queen just takes and White has the
same problem).

Then

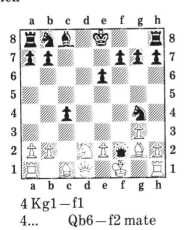

4 Kg1—f1
4...   Qb6—f2 mate

The king cannot get to g1 or e1
because of the black queen.

The king cannot take the queen
as it is protected by that knight.

What Veitch played:

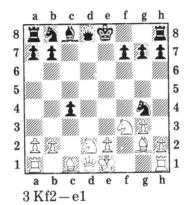

3 Kf2—e1

Veitch saw what would happen with
the other moves, so he played his
king back to e1.

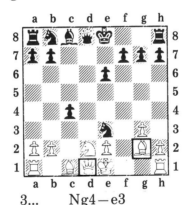

3...   Ng4—e3

The knight forks the queen and the
bishop.

But the knight is only after the
big fish...the queen.

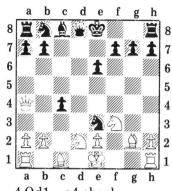

4 Qd1 — a4 check

This check was the only square
Veitch's queen could safely go to.
Unfortunately not for long.

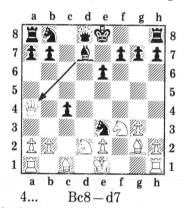

4...   Bc8 — d7

The bishop blocks the check and
attacks the queen.

What now for the queen?
Say

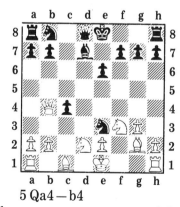

5 Qa4 — b4

The queen moves on one of the only
two squares where it is not
attacked.

Now the knight

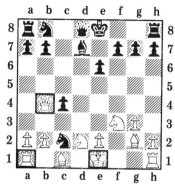

5...   Ne3 — c2 check

The knight makes a family fork!
King, rook and queen are all
included. After the king moves,
young Jonathan Penrose would
obviously take the queen.

In the game Walter Veitch saw
the damage that would be done
after he had played his king back to
e1, and he resigned. A beautiful
game.

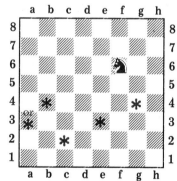

This is the journey of Penrose's
knight.

Some knight! Some journey!

A Lincolnshire
junior event

A Game for you to try

Pawns on the starting grid with white bishop at c1 and black knight at b8.

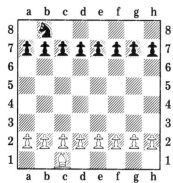

*The rule for this game: the first to get a pawn through to the far row wins; however the pawn must not be captured immediately following arrival.

I am not going to finish this game though; it is up to you to do that.

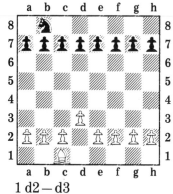

1 d2 — d3

Put your pawns on squares of the opposite colour to the bishop. If you block your bishop with pawns you will very soon have a lost game.

Look for moves which limit the knight.

The knight in this diagram would be taken by a pawn if it moved forward.

So move the bishop — and block the knight.

You could also try

*Knights with the pawn teams.

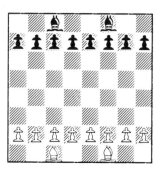

*Bishops with the pawn teams.

The Bishop is good too!

Bishop forks the king and the rook. White must move the king out of check and then the bishop skates back for the rook.

The bishop checks the king.

After the king moves the bishop will go through and take the queen.

The bishop attacks the knight which cannot move, as that would leave the king in check. Next move the bishop will take the knight.

The Rook

Why do we call the castle a rook? We think that chess began in India and the word 'rukh' meant chariot. The Arabs, when they started their conquests spread the game, and chess sets sold in Europe by Parsee Indians pictured the rook as a tower carried by an elephant. So many languages simply called it a tower or a castle.

The rook is the flying winger of the chess board. He moves in straight lines. But he cannot move on diagonals. Move the rook up and down the board and feel its speed and power. Let it sweep across the squares.

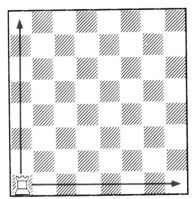

A Rook exercise

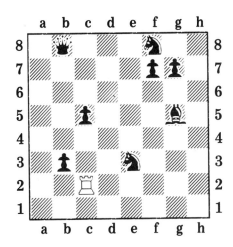

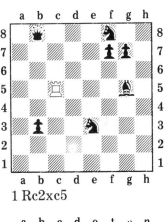

1 Rc2xc5

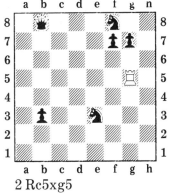

2 Rc5xg5

You have 8 moves with the white rook. The black pieces are fixed and do not move. Can you take everything on the board? Watch the move by move demonstration and then come back and see if you can do it yourself.

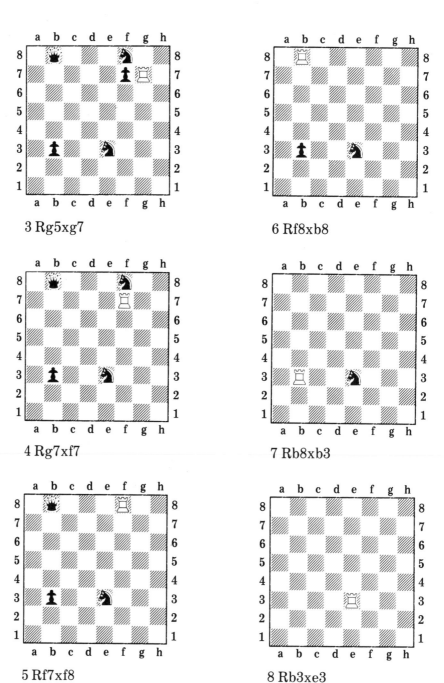

3 Rg5xg7

6 Rf8xb8

4 Rg7xf7

7 Rb8xb3

5 Rf7xf8

8 Rb3xe3
Now you go back and see how
quickly you can do it.

The Rook that grinds like a mill

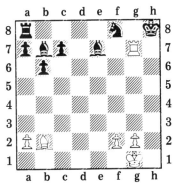

Just watch the rook on g7 take everything on the seventh rank and the rook on a8.

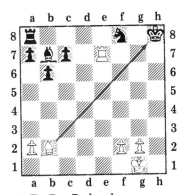

1 Rg7xe7 check

This is called 'discovered check'. The rook has moved and we discover that the king is in check from the bishop on b2.

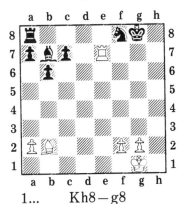

1... Kh8—g8

This is the king's only move, and on this discovered check the whole pattern of the next few moves depends.

The rook has already taken a bishop.

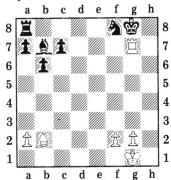

2 Re7—g7 check

The rook goes back to manoeuvre the king into the corner for a further discovered check.

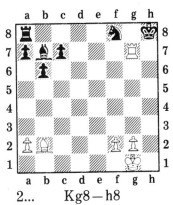

2... Kg8—h8

The king is now on the diagonal of the bishop and the rook has a free dangerous move.

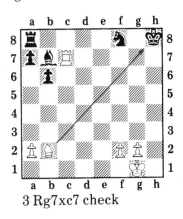

3 Rg7xc7 check

The free move! The king is in check
from that bishop again.

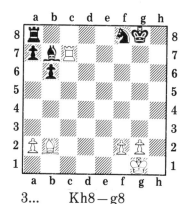

3...   Kh8−g8

The king escapes to the only
available square.

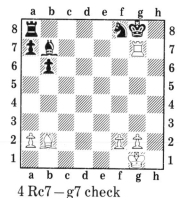

4 Rc7−g7 check

The rook returns to check, forcing
the king back onto that long
diagonal where the bishop is.
    The bishop does the checking.
    The rook just grinds away.

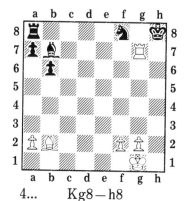

4...   Kg8−h8

Now for that free move.

Which one would you make?

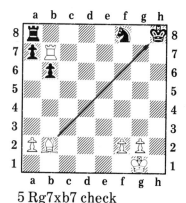

5 Rg7xb7 check

Yes, why not take the bishop?
    After all, the king is in check
from the bishop.

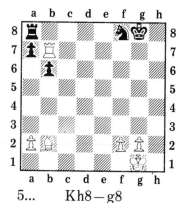

5...   Kh8−g8

The king does his usual.

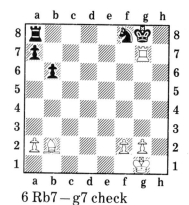

6 Rb7−g7 check

The check comes: the king has to go
to h8.

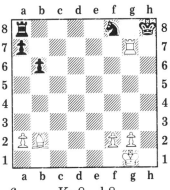

London junior
Julian Hodgson

6...   Kg8 — h8

Another free move! Why not take another pawn?

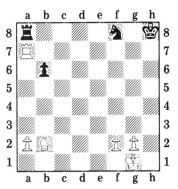

7 Rg7xa7 check

This also attacks white's rook.

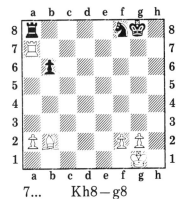

7...   Kh8 — g8

But next move White takes the rook getting a position like this.

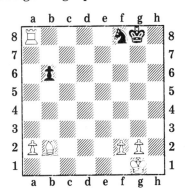

8 Ra7xa8

Now White has a position with king, rook and bishop and pawns against king, knight and pawn.

This is a very big advantage.

Can you grind like a mill?

Can you get with your rook on g7 to the enemy's rook on a8, taking the queen on d7, the pawn on c7, the knight on b7 and the pawn on a7 on the way?

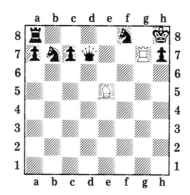

Another game for you to try

Try the rook and pawn teams.

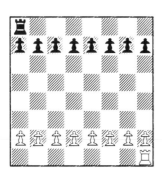

And beware of this.

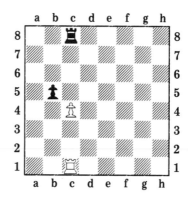

Should the white pawn at c4 take the black pawn? Perhaps you remember something from the queen games.

The white pawn is pinned because of Rc8xRc1.

Mating Races

One of the most popular games is the mating race. Can you achieve a checkmate quicker than your friend?

Both of you are given the same pieces, the same position. First, one of you tries to give checkmate, then the other. The winner is the one who completes the checkmate in the least number of moves. First we show you two rooks building up and tightening a mating net.

Two Rooks v King

This is one we will show you, but when you do this checkmate little snags may crop up — but this is the pattern you could do it by;

The start position of the race. Afterwards see if you can do it any quicker.

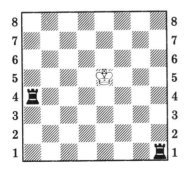

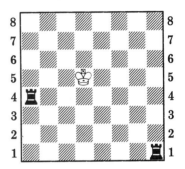

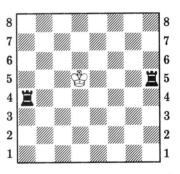

Two rooks work together, one checking — the other cutting off ranks 1-4.

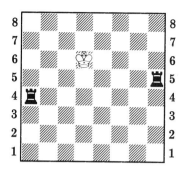

The king is now forced back.

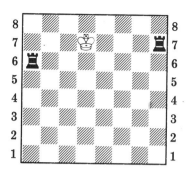

Now his field is even more roped off. He has only rank 8 left.

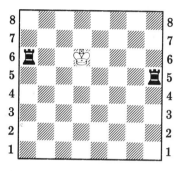

Now ranks 1-6 are cut off to the king.

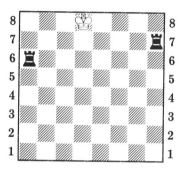

He cannot hide now.

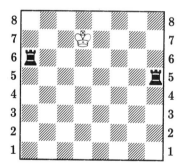

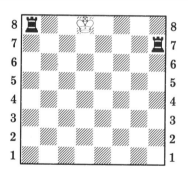

There is nowhere left to go. It's mate! Could you?

Exercises

We set two mating races for you to try.

How many moves do you need as Black to give checkmate? And your friend? I took five.

If you have just the king, then you will make it harder for your opponent with the two rooks if you take your king across to attack one of the rooks.

Black moves first. Only count his moves.

The attacking forces have here 50 moves to mate; otherwise it is a draw.

I reckon it should take four.

King and two bishops v King

Here is another one for you to try. Watch the demonstration and then see if you can do it. Then see if your friend can beat you in doing it. Remember the argument over the bishop and the knight and which one was better. Perhaps it ought to be pointed out that, while king and two bishops can force checkmate, the king and two knights cannot:

Sure this is checkmate, but your opponent would have to play one careless move to allow it.

Two bishops can force checkmate.

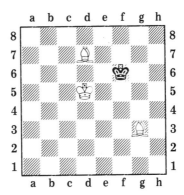

The idea you have to keep in your head is to drive the black king into the corner.

You will be able to see how the
bishops imprison the king in the
corner.

This is check and the king is
forced to retreat.

1 Bg3 — h4 check

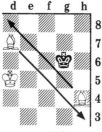

1...   Kf6 — g6

It's rather like a force field, isn't it?
There's no crossing the fire of the
two bishops.

2 Kd5 — e5

You need your king to help in the
finish.

2...   Kg6 — f7

The black king paces around in his
cage of nine squares.

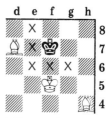

3 Ke5 — f5

The white king takes away one of
those squares. Which?

Yes, it's g6.

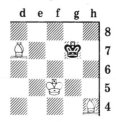

3...   Kf7 — g7

What better?

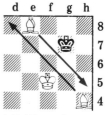

4 Bd7 — e8

White seizes another diagonal.
Black's king is limited to six
squares in the corner.

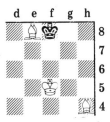

4...   Kg7—f8

King attacks bishop.

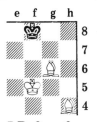

5 Be8—g6

Black's corner is down to five
squares.

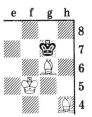

5...   Kf8—g7

He stays out of the corner as long as
possible.

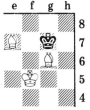

6 Bh4—e7

Black's corner patch has shrunk to
four squares.

Now, to which square should the
black king be moved? h6? g8? h8?
Think. Which is best?
    Which is safest?

Not to h6? White's bishop at e7
would go to f8, checkmate.

6...   Kg7—g8

Best. Stay out of the corner.

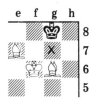

7 Kf5—f6

This hems the black king into two
squares — g8 and h8.

7...   Kg8—h8

Only move.
    Do not reduce the black king's
area to one square. That would be
stalemate. Be careful.

What exactly are we trying to do? What mating position do we want to reach?

This is one possibility.

How can we achieve such a position? Let's organise an improvement in the position of the white king. It'll take two moves.

8 Bg6 — f5

The bishop vacates g6 square for his king.

8...   Kh8 — g8

Must.

9 Kf6 — g6

The white king controls h7, g7 and f7.

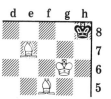

9...   Kg8 — h8

Perhaps White will now play 10 Bf5 — e6 stalemating?

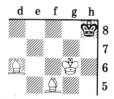

10 Be7 — d6

Deliberately waiting.

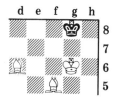

10...   Kh8 — g8

No fun.

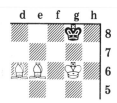

11 Bf5 — e6 check

In for the kill.

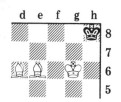

11...   Kg8 — h8

No comment.

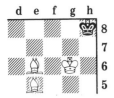

12 Bd6 — e5 mate
The king is dead.

Now you can go back to the starting position and do these checkmates in fewer moves than your friend. Start with the two rooks.

A hard one. Can you remember?

King and rook v king. A hard one. To help you we show you some rook checkmates.

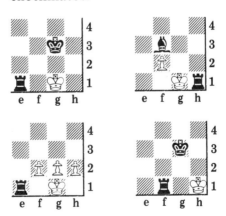

Full Board

Bank holiday. The market place was crowded except for the roped-off space in its heart. Banners fluttered in the breeze. The works band played a brisk medley. The mayor, chains and all, sat high above the throng in a tennis umpire's chair placed on the side nearest the town hall steps. The town football club's manager, surrounded by fans, sat facing him across the space which was marked out as a giant chessboard. Six young trumpeters stood poised across the High St. entrance. Behind them could be seen costumed live chess pieces lining up for a stylish entrance.

The master of ceremony raised his finger. The trumpets blared forth. The procession started to move. A little boy plucked nervously at the mayor's robe. 'The board's the wrong way round.' The mayor looked at the nearest right hand corner square. He went pale. It was black. He looked at the town engineer. 'Does it matter?' 'It's the rule, sir. Players must have white corner squares nearest their right hands.' He gestured to the traffic warden who raised her hand and stopped the procession. The mayor

climbed down from his seat. 'Shift the chairs to those sides quickly, please.'

Once more the trumpets rang forth. The TV cameras ran. The procession moved forward.

First, riding on motor cycles, came four rooks, two with white castle-like structures round them, two with black. They were directed to the corner squares.

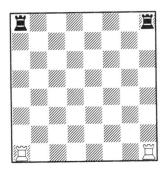

Four knights on horses were then guided by their squires to the squares next to the rooks.

The four bishops walked in solemn single file to the centre of the board before dispersing to squares next to the knights.

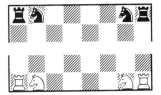

Another fanfare. The black queen appeared in a small sports car. The traffic warden looked uncertain as to which of the two remaining squares she should direct her. The football manager spoke into his microphone. 'The queen always starts on a square of her own colour. Black queen — black square.' Cheers.

Trumpets again. This time the local beauty queen — in white — was driven in her white sports car to her white square.

More trumpeting. The black king, robed, attended by pages, strides to the remaining back row square. His forces bow.

Trumpets. The white king makes his entry, takes up his station and acknowledges the salutes.

Trumpets. Eight black pawns and eight white pawns march in on to the second rows next to their pieces.

The game is ready to start. The ambulance men and police move to the wings ready to remove the battle casualties. The band plays the national anthem. The public address system comes once more to life. The crowd hushes.

Mayors always make first moves. White always starts first. The mayor makes his move. 'My 'e'-pawn two squares forward, please.'

The game went on its way. The charity collectors rattled their boxes. Finally the board was cleared of all but the two kings. An honourable draw.

Check list:
Right-hand corner white
Rooks, Knights, Bishops.
Queen on own colour.
King. Pawns.
White begins.

Four-Move Checkmate

This is something to beware of when you start playing chess. If you are not careful, your enemy's queen and bishop can finish the game in four moves. If an Arab from the court of Haroun al Rashid, one of the famous Caliphs of Bagdad, travelled through time to see the modern game, this is one of the things that would most shock him. For his queen — only to him it was a minister not a queen — moved only one square diagonally. His bishop moved two squares diagonally. But, whereas the Arab took ages to get to grips with his opponents at chess, here in four flashing moves is checkmate. No wonder the knights of the middle ages called the new queen 'Mad'. This four-move checkmate is something you must know. This is how it goes.

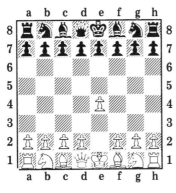

1 e2 — e4

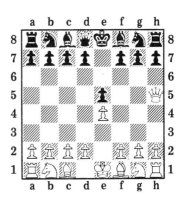

2 Qd1 — h5

A beginner's move.

This early queen sortie is not recommended, even though it may lead to wins against the other beginners.

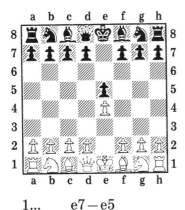

1...   e7 — e5

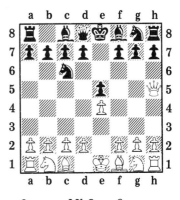

2...   Nb8 — c6

73

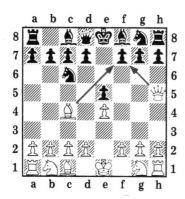

3 Bf1 — c4

Now queen and bishop attack the weak spot f7.

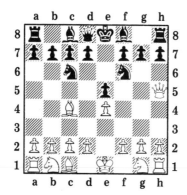

3...   Ng8 — f6

Black fails to spot White's idea.

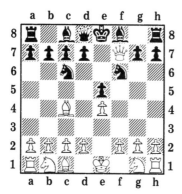

4 Qh5xf7

Checkmate. The game is already over!

Good players easily block this attack.

Let us try.

How to stop the 'Mad' Queen
A feeble attempt

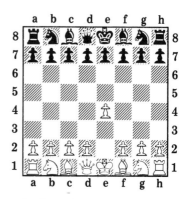

1 e2 — e4

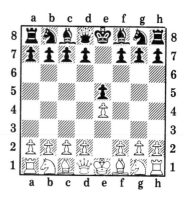

1...   e7 — e5

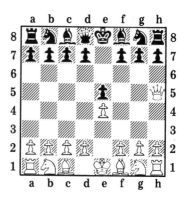

2 Qd1 — h5

Black's f7 pawn is the main target.

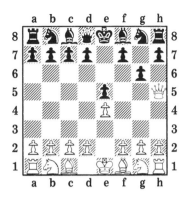

2...   g7 — g6??

This could have waited. White's queen has a second target.

3...   Qd8-e7

The queen blocks the check.

3 Qh5xe5 check

This gives check and the queen also attacks the rook on h8.

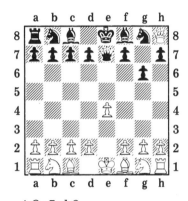

4 Qe5xh8

White has made a good start.

A better defence

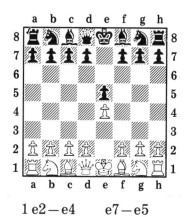

1 e2 — e4   e7 — e5

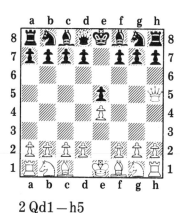

2 Qd1 — h5

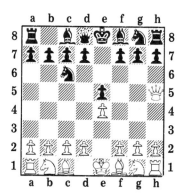

2...   Nb8 — c6
Protect that pawn this time.

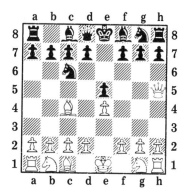

3 Bf1 — c4
Out comes the bishop. Is it to be
mate next move?

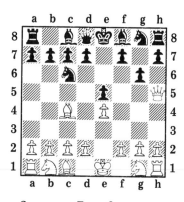

3...   g7 — g6
Okay now as all Black's pawns are
protected.

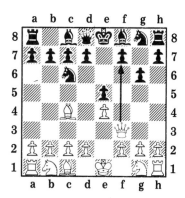

4 Qh5 — f3
Retreat is the order of the day. But
checkmate by Qxf7 is still
threatened.

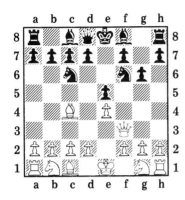

4...   Ng8—f6

Black blocks the path of the white queen and stops the mate.

Black has many good opening plans that avoid the four-move checkmate. Here is one:—

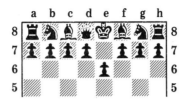

Black, on his first move, plays
        1...   e7—e6.

And, on the second move, follows up with
        2...   d7—d5.

Two Last Rules

Castling

Now that we know the moves of the king and rook it is time to tell you the one last move there is to learn. In the middle ages the chessplayers found out that the king occasionally needed a leap to safety in a corner.

In the 14th and 15th centuries 'castling' was introduced. This and the new move of the 'mad queen' added new powers of speed and movement to the game. What, then, is castling?

When you 'castle' you do two things. First you play your king two squares along the back row towards a rook. Then you leap that rook over the king on to the next square. This all counts as one move.

You can castle towards either rook.

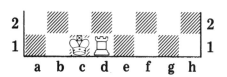

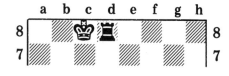

You cannot castle

1 If the king or the rook has moved.

2 If there is a piece between the king and the rook.

3 While the king is in check.

4 If the king ends up in check.

5 If the king passes through check. This is a difficult one and here are four examples.

Do you understand this difficult rule now?

Castling can be a good idea. The king is put into safety in a corner of the board. The rook is brought into the action.

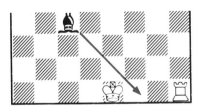

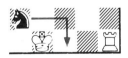

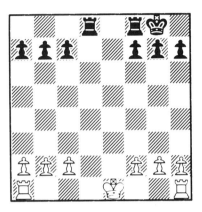

Start.

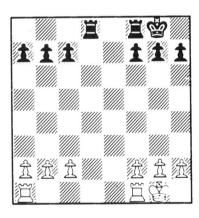

What a good idea castling is!

'En passant'

There is one final rule for you to understand about — a special pawn move. It was made to stop the game becoming blocked by pawn barriers.

This is the rule. When you move your pawn two squares I have the privilege of pushing it back one square and taking it, if I am able, with one of my own pawns. But I must do it on the immediately following move.

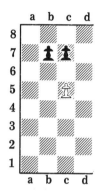

If black advances his 'b'-pawn one square, the white pawn can take it.

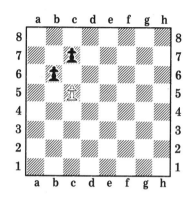

Now I push his pawn back one square to b6.

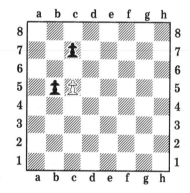

The 'b'-pawn advances two squares from b7 — b5. My 'c'-pawn can still take it! But I must do this next move.

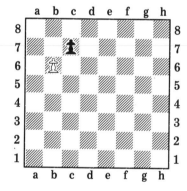

Then, as part of the same move, I take it.

Repeat

His pawn moves two squares.

Next move, I push it back one so that my pawn can and does take it.

Mating Nets

Progressive chess

Here is another game which is fun to try and can teach you how to build mating nets around opponents' kings.

In this game White has one move, then Black has two moves in a row, then White three moves, Black four...and so on.

Two rules: you can give check only on the last of your series of moves; you must get out of check on the first of the series.

A sample game:

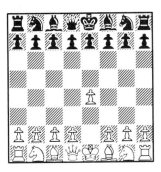

White has played e2 — e4.

White, having three moves, played Bf1 — c4, Qd1 — h5 and Qh5xf7 checkmate — our old friend the four move checkmate.

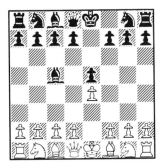

Black, with two moves, played e7 — e5 and Bf8 — c5.

Lost on a train journey

Bob Wade lost the following game on a train journey in Canada.

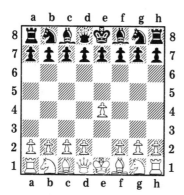

White plays e2—e4.

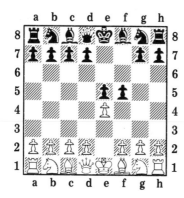

Black (2 moves) plays e7—e5 and f7—f5.

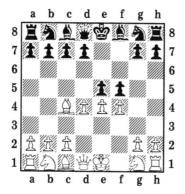

White (3 moves) plays d2—d4, f2—f4 and Bf1—c4.

Now we shall stop at this position. Can Black bring the queen to f2 in four moves, protected by a bishop or knight, to give checkmate? Unfortunately only by bringing the queen through h4 where it gives check before the last move. But Black can give checkmate in another way!

Can you see how to bring this about?

Black must cover the white king's escape squares d2, e2, f2 and f1 to prepare the checkmate.

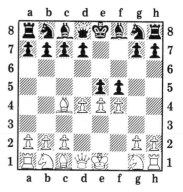

Only the queen will be able to cover these squares quickly enough. Where must the queen go to watch over all these four squares? It has to go to g2.

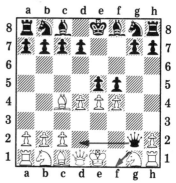

Black plays Qd8—g5 and Qg5xg2 using two of his four moves.

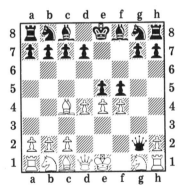

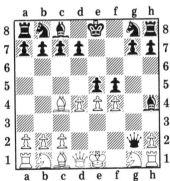

What piece can give check and mate on the last two moves?

The bishop on f8 can check on b4, but, as White can block the diagonal, that's no good. But the bishop can mate! Bring it to h4. Black plays Bf8—e7 and Be7—h4.

The king has no escape squares because of the queen at g2; the checking bishop cannot be blocked; so it is checkmate.

A Complete Game

By playing through the many beautiful games of Paul Morphy you will get a great feel for sound attacking chess. Here is one worthy game in which Paul was Black against John Schulten.

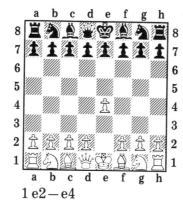

1 e2 — e4

Bobby Fischer likes this best too.

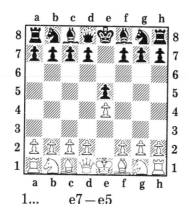

1...   e7 — e5

Good for Black as well.

2 f2 — f4

This move deliberately gives a pawn. Such gifts at the beginning of a game are called gambits. This one is called the King's Gambit. White wants to have his two centre pawns free to advance into the heart of Black's position.

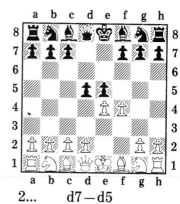

2...   d7 — d5

Morphy gives one too! He wants his queen and 'c'-bishop in play. When Black gives a pawn as well, this is called a 'counter-gambit.'

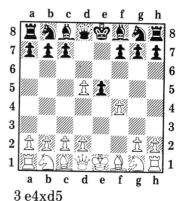

3 e4xd5

White takes one of the pawns.

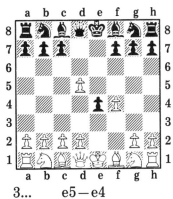

3...   e5 — e4

The black pawn comes deep into
White's position.

4 Nb1 — c3

The knight now attacks the
dangerous black pawn and defends
the pawn on d5.

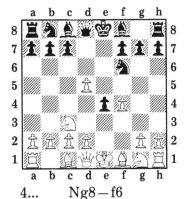

4...   Ng8 — f6

The black knight comes out. It
defends the advanced pawn.

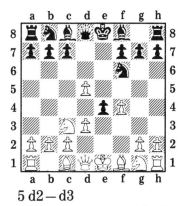

5 d2 — d3

White wants rid of the black pawn.

5...   Bf8 — b4

This move pins the knight which
now cannot move as the white king
would be left in check. Now, of
course, this knight cannot help in
the centre.

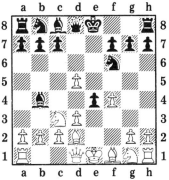

6 Bc1 — d2

Unpinning. The knight is now free
to move.

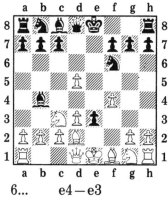

6...   e4 — e3

A Morphy move! He wants to open the 'e'-line and attack down it.

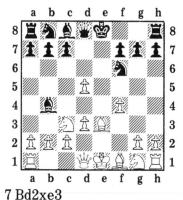

7 Bd2xe3

Of course! But notice the knight is now pinned again.

7...   0 — 0

Black castles and is ready now to put his rook on the same file as the white king. He already has more pieces out than White.

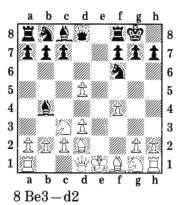

8 Be3 — d2

The bishop unpins the knight (again!).

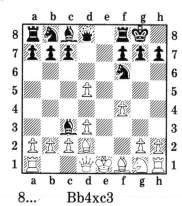

8...   Bb4xc3

This knight is taken off so it cannot block the wide open king-line at e4 or e2.

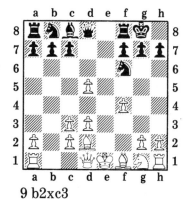

9 b2xc3

Pawn recaptures.

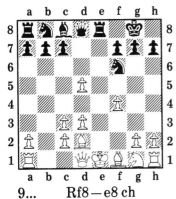

9...   Rf8 — e8 ch

'Ch' is for check.

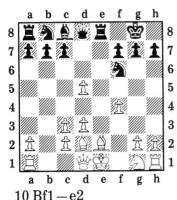

10 Bf1 — e2

The bishop shields the king.

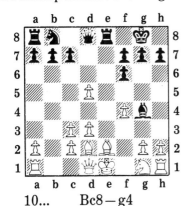

10...   Bc8 — g4

The black bishop stalks out, confident that it cannot be taken.

Why not? White's bishop is pinned against the king.

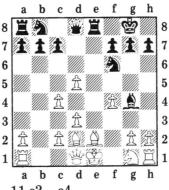

11 c3 — c4

White tries to keep his extra pawns, but it's a bad idea. Better to bring the sleeping pieces off the back rank into action.

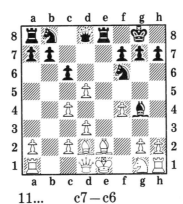

11...   c7 — c6

Morphy now wants the queen-file open and his other knight in play.

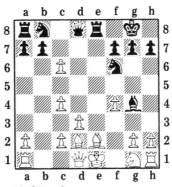

12 d5xc6

White stays two pawns ahead.

But Black's knight is brought into the attack.

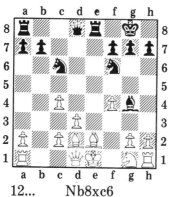

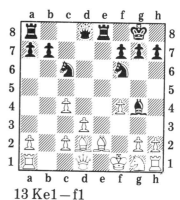

12...   Nb8xc6

13 Ke1 — f1

The master has a problem — from a "simultaneous" in a Russian park

Now the threat is...Nc6 — d4 making the attack on the king even stronger. It is now difficult for White to find any good defence.

The king gets off the danger line, but it is too late.

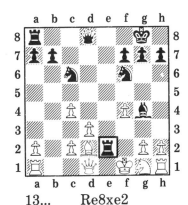

13... Re8xe2

Bang! One white defender, the bishop, says adieu.

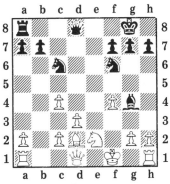

14 Ng1xe2

White has to capture with the knight. If he captured with the queen, the bishop of course would take it.

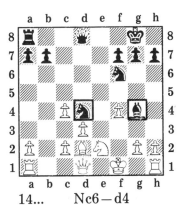

14... Nc6—d4

The knight comes in to help sure in the knowledge that White cannot afford to take it. Why not? He would lose his queen.

Yet another 'pin'.

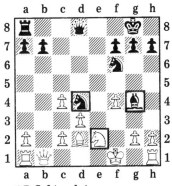

15 Qd1—b1

The queen moves out of the way. She cannot save the menaced white knight.

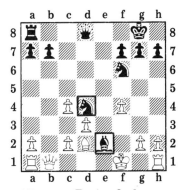

15... Bg4xe2 ch

The black bishop snaps up the unprotected knight and gives check.

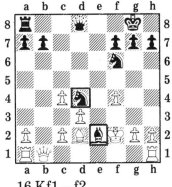

16 Kf1—f2

The king's life is now short.
  All moves lead to checkmate.

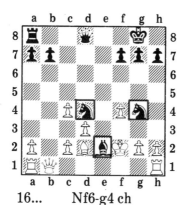

16...   Nf6-g4 ch

Another black piece comes giving check!

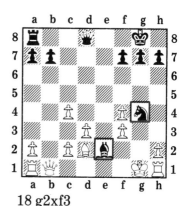

18 g2xf3

Captures the knight — and now beware!

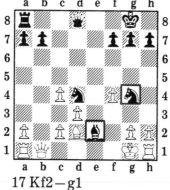

17 Kf2−g1

The white king hides in the corner. The white king and queen block their own rooks.

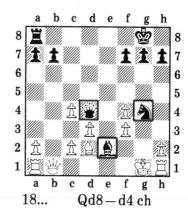

18...   Qd8−d4 ch

In comes the queen!

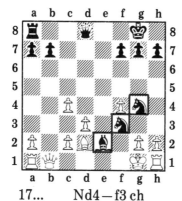

17...   Nd4−f3 ch

Again giving check but really making way for the deadly black queen.

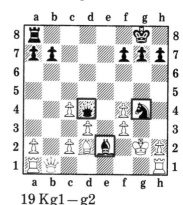

19 Kg1−g2

It's the only move.

*London Junior
Championships*

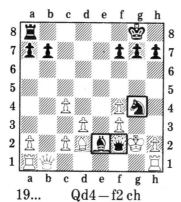

19...   Qd4 — f2 ch

The black queen strikes into the heart of the white defence and gives check.

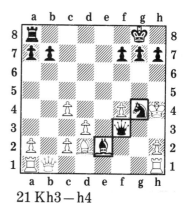

21 Kh3 — h4

The king migrates further north. It'll get cold up there!

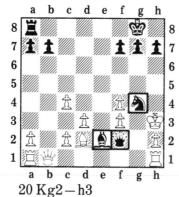

20 Kg2 — h3

The king escapes — but not far.

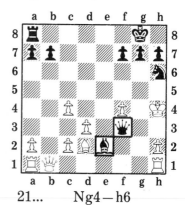

21...   Ng4 — h6

The knight frees g4 to allow the queen to checkmate.

20...   Qf2xf3 ch

check again.

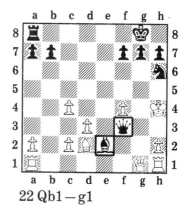

22 Qb1 — g1

The white queen makes its second move of the game.

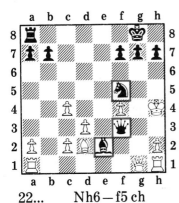

22...   Nh6 — f5 ch

The knight gives the last but one check.

23...   Qf3 — h5

Checkmate. The king is dead!

Morphy has played the attack with every move counting.

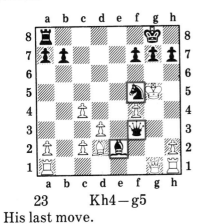

23   Kh4 — g5

His last move.

Half a Point is Better than None

If you can't win, you need not lose. You can draw, shake hands and share the honours. In chess we score 1 point for a win, ½ for a draw and 0 for a loss.

Perhaps if you both play perfectly the game must be drawn. To finish up even after a hard battle must be more satisfying than beating a weak opponent.

Here are some endings which are drawn. You cannot give checkmate.

King versus King
Obviously a draw.

The bishop giving check cannot also control the neighbouring squares g8 and h7. The white king cannot be next to the black king and therefore cannot cover both h7 and g8.

King and knight against king. Stalemate. If the knight controls a neighbouring square it cannot also give check.

As this shows, the two knights can give checkmate. But it cannot be forced. The opponent must help. Last move the black king went the wrong way. With best play the king and two knights only draw.

You agree a draw in such cases. In fact you can agree a draw any time during the game.

How else do we make draws?
There's stalemate.
There's the 50 move rule.
There's repeating the position three times.

Stalemate

When you have an overwhelming force and this happens you'll feel a fool.

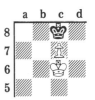
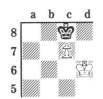

White to move. If he plays Kd6 — c6 Black is stalemated. With any other legal move he has to say goodbye to his pawn, and king versus king is a draw to be agreed.

There are many who think that to give stalemate should count as a win. But that's not in the rules.

Sometimes stalemate is the logical end to a game.

50-Move Rule

Either player can claim a draw if nothing happens on the chessboard for 50 moves by each. But captures or pawn moves are happenings which mean that the counting must restart.

Repeated Position

Even the great players get this rule wrong. So it's worth getting clear from the start.

The rule — if the identical position (same pieces on same squares, same player to move) has happened or is about to happen three times, the one, whose turn it is to move, may claim a draw.

This rule is confusing because the repetitions do not have to be in a row.

Perpetual check, which means checking forever, is a form of repetition. Examples:

The white rook will give check on h7 and g7 for ever. The black king can only go back and fro between h8 and g8.

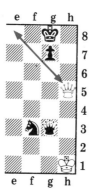

Black has a knight and pawn more but the white queen gives perpetual check by Qh5 — e8 and Qe8 — h5 and the black king can only to and fro between g8 and h7.

In the 21 games of the famous world championship match in 1972 between Boris Spassky and Bobby Fischer five games were drawn because of repeated positions, two of these being by perpetual check.

Prodigies at Play

Abe Yanofsky

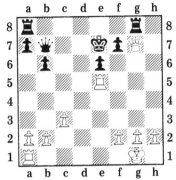

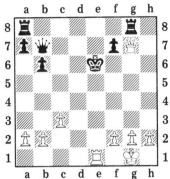

Fourteen-year-old Abe Yanofsky, playing for Canada in the 1939 Olympiad, was faced with problems in this position. If he moves his attacked queen off the 'g'-file, Black mates by ...Qb7xg2.

Black's 'f'-pawn is pinned and cannot take. Black played 1... Ke7xe6 and White brought his rook into the attack by 2 Ra1-e1 ch.

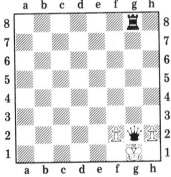

The answer he found was to drive the black king into the open by 1 Re5xe6 ch

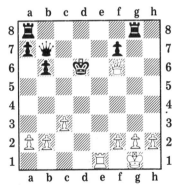

Black played 2... Ke6 — d6, and White checked with 3 Qg7 — f6.

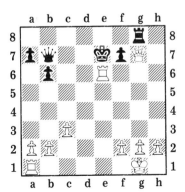

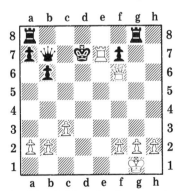

If the black king had retreated by 3... Kd6 — d7 White has 4 Re1 — e7 ch attacking the black king

and queen on the same line. Such an attack is called a "skewer". Black would lose his queen for the white rook.

Black hopefully played 3... Kd6 − d5 and White continued his attack with 4 Re1 − e5 ch, forcing 4...Kd5 − c4.

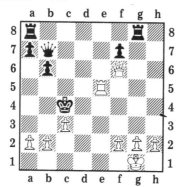

Abe now played 5 b2 − b3 ch and finished the game after

5...	Kc4 − d3
6 Qf6 − d6ch	Kd3 − c2
7 Re5 − e2ch	Kc2 − c1
8 Qd6 − d2ch	Kc1 − b1
9 Qd2 − d1 checkmate	

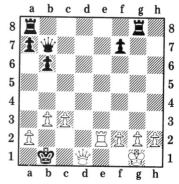

Black's still waiting to give checkmate on g2.

Bobby Fischer

In January 1958, Bobby Fischer won the US championship. This led to him playing in a world championship qualifying tournament in September and he came in the top 6, and that put Bobby in the world's top 9! He automatically became a grandmaster, the youngest ever.

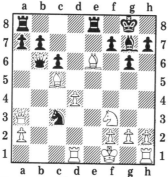

This position, taken from the Game of the Century, the title given to a

game won by Fischer when he was 13, formed a small but vital part of his calculations.

He planned to play 1...Qb6 − b5 check, which would lead to checkmate.

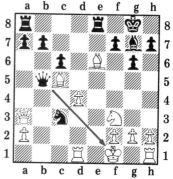

If White plays 2 Kf1 − e1 Black has a simple mate by 2... Qb5 − e2, the queen being protected by the knight:

White must play 2 Kf1 — g1.

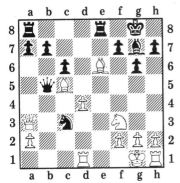

Black would now continue
2...Nc3 — e2 ch.

forcing 3 Kg1 — f1

Now look carefully. White king and
black queen are on the same
diagonal. Any knight move would
give discovered check. With mate in
mind Bobby would have played
3...Ne2 — g3 double check.

*Bobby Fischer in
championship play*

White's best is 4 Kf1-g1.

99

Now Bobby would have played the stunning 4...Qb5 — f1 ch. He would lose a queen but get a checkmate.

The king cannot capture. White must play 5 Rd1xf1.

Now would come 5...Ng3 — e2 mate! This is a smothered mate. The white king is smothered by its own pieces.

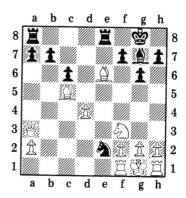

The Younger Set

Nigel Short

When Nigel Short was 12 he was
already a very experienced
tournament player.

No one, watching Nigel's game
with Max Fuller at the Charlton
Open Tournament in the Summer of
1977, was surprised when Max as
Black resigned in this position.

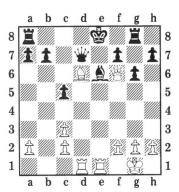

Vasily Smyslov and Nigel Short go over their game once more

Max must keep his queen placed to stop Nigel playing Qf6—e7 checkmate.

Nigel threatens to play 1 Bd6xc5 uncovering his rook on to the black queen and after 1...Qd7—c7 Nigel would give checkmate after 2 Re1 x e6 ch, f7 x e6, 3 Qf6 x e6 ch, Qc7—e7, by 4 Qe6 x e7.

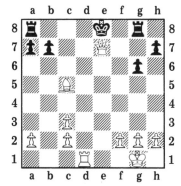

No move seemed to offer Max any prospect of rescue. He knew he was up against a highly experienced 12 year-old veteran. There was not the slightest chance of Nigel going wrong.

The moves of the game, given in a short form of algebraic notation in which only the piece's arrival square is mentioned, were:

White: Nigel Short
Black: Max Fuller

1 e4	c5
2 Nf3	Nc6
3 Bb5	Qb6
4 Bxc6	Qxc6
5 0—0	g6
6 Nc3	Bg7
7 d4	d6
8 dxc5	dxc5
9 Bf4	Bxc3
10 bxc3	Qxe4
11 Qc1	Bf5
12 Re1	Qa4
13 Qe3	Qc6
14 Ne5	Qc8
15 Nc4	Be6
16 Qe5	Nf6
17 Nd6 ch	exd6
18 Qxf6	Rg8
19 Bxd6	Qd7
20 Rad1	Black resigned

Two months later, Nigel was playing in the British championship final tournament, easily the youngest player to have qualified. He beat Dr Penrose, the ten times former holder, and had a rating performance from his eleven games of 200 (2,200 on the International Scale).

Ex-world champion Vasily Smyslov is playing a number of young players simultaneously

Joel Benjamin

Joel Benjamin, at the time of writing this book, is the youngest American to reach the rating norm of 2,200 (= England's 200) — at the age of 13 years 3 months, two months younger than Bobby Fischer achieved it.

Joel was White in this position taken from a game he played in the 1976 US Open Championship (Joel was then 12). See how his opponent's pieces are clustered on the wing away from his king. Joel finished off the game in grown-up fashion by bringing another piece into the attack against black's king. He played 1 Rd1 — d3 preparing to place the rook at g3 or h3. The game went 1...Kg8 — h7 2 f6xg7 Qc7 — e7 3 Rd3 — h3.

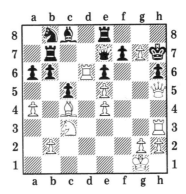

His opponent resigned as he cannot stop Joel from playing Qh5xh6 and quickly checkmating, 3...Qe7 — g5 would not help Black as White would reply Qh5xg5 knowing that Black could not recapture — Blacks 'h'-pawn must remain on the 'h'-file to shelter its king.

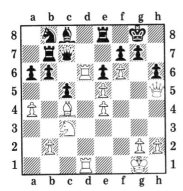

Gary Kasparov

Gary Kasparov, the USSR's 14-year-old junior champion won this game in a telex match USSR — Australia in 1977.

White: Gary Kasparov
Black: Guy West

1 e2 — e4	c7 — c5
2 Ng1 — f3	Ng8 — f6
3 Nb1 — c3	e7 — e6
4 d2 — d4	c5xd4
5 Nf3xd4	Bf8 — b4
6 e4 — e5	

Attacking the knight

6 ...	Nf6 — d5
7 Bc1 — d2	Nd5xc3
8 b2xc3	Bb4 — f8
9 Bf1 — d3	d7 — d6
10 Qd1 — e2	

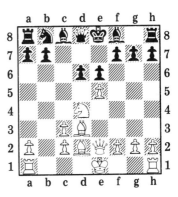

Gary Kasparov

White has moved more pieces off the back row and into play and must have the better chances of winning.

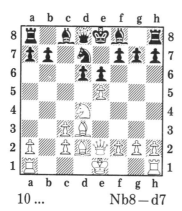

10 ...   Nb8—d7

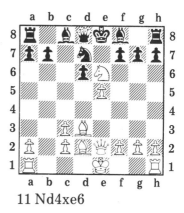

11 Nd4xe6

This knight's trespassing.

It's got the cheek to attack the black queen.

What happens if Guy takes it?

104

After
  11 ...   f7xe6
Gary would unleash the attacking team of queen, two bishops and advanced pawn by 12 Qe2—h5 ch. The black king is open.

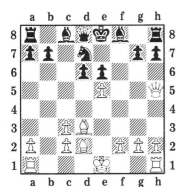

The game could then go
  12...   g7—g6
  13 Bd3xg6 ch   h7xg6
  14 Qh5xg6 ch
driving the black king to e7 after which Gary would have skewered the black king and queen by
  15 Bd2—g5 ch
inflicting heavy material loss.

  Guy West didn't like that possibility. He did not take the knight but moved his attacked queen to square b6.

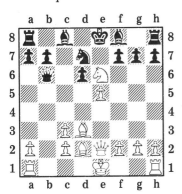

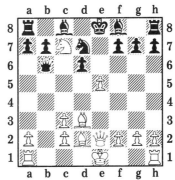

Gary played
  12 Ne6—c7
checking the black king and attacking a rook.

You look carefully at the position.
  You see that West can play queen takes knight. Imagine he does.

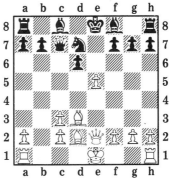

Gary would play 13 e5xd6 with 'discovered check' (as we say).

The black king is attacked by the queen and must be saved. The white pawn is attacking Black's queen. That queen is lost. Guy resigned the game.

Maya Chiburdanidze, *right*, 16 year old girl from Georgia (USSR), won her way to the women's world championship final in 1978.

More Famous Young Players

Elaine Saunders (now Mrs Pritchard) won the British Ladies Championship in 1939 when she was only 13 years old.

Henrique Mecking was 13 when he became champion of Brazil and 14 when he shared first place in the 1966 South American qualifying tournament for the world championship. Now he's regarded as one of the world's top ten.

Sammy Reshevsky, playing in a strong New York tournament in 1922, then only 10 years of age, beat David Janowski, former challenger for the world championship. In 1948 Reshevsky was himself third in the world championship tournament. When only 8 he was touring chess clubs to play simultaneously on many boards.

Mecking at Hastings, England

Arturo Pomar, *right*, many times Spanish champion, was champion of the Balearic Islands when he was 11. In 1944, two years later he drew a very hard game with Dr Alekhine, the world champion, after coming close to winning the game.

How Good a Player are You?

Score and grade your own tournament

You (John) organise a tournament with your friends Bill, Ann and Sam. You all play one game against each other.

Round one
>   John and Ann had a stalemate — draw.
>   Sam beat Bill

Round two
>   Ann drew with Sam
>   John beat Bill

Round three
>   Bill beat Ann
>   Sam beat John

Score 1 point for a win, ½ for a draw and 0 for a loss. Here is the score table:

	John	Ann	Bill	Sam	Total
John meets	X	½	1	0	1½
Ann meets	½	X	0	½	1
Bill meets	0	1	X	0	1
Sam meets	1	½	1	X	2½

Sam is the winner.

Let's grade your results just as English club players do.

Basically you should be 50 grading points at least better than anyone you can always beat.

The system

If you win, take your opponent's grade and add 50.
If you lose, take your opponent's grade and subtract 50.
If you draw, take your opponent's grade.

The average of all these results is your grade. But you must not lose grading points by winning nor gain points by losing. Don't count such results.

You can build up an approximate unofficial grade if one of your players, say John, has a grade through playing in schools leagues. Say John is 75. After some juggling of figures I would make Sam about 110, Ann 65, Bill 60 and John 75.

Do you want to convert your national grading (official or unofficial) into the international scale used in USA and by world chess. Multiply your 'English' figure by 8 and then add 600.

Sam 110 x 8 = 880 + 600 = 1480
Ann 65 x 8 = 520 + 600 = 1120
Bill 60 x 8 = 480 + 600 = 1080
John 75 x 8 = 600 + 600 = 1200

Have a look to see how you compare with world champions Capablanca and Karpov in the Prodigy Chart prepared by Len Barden, England's manager of junior training.

You and your friends can have your own rating system.

Age progress

	1500	1600	1700	1800	1900	2000	2100	2200	2300
World Champions									
Morphy									
Steinitz									
Lasker									
Capablanca						12	13	13	17
Alekhine						14	14	14	14
Euwe						14		16	18
Botvinnik						13	13	13	13
Spassky		9	10	10	11	11	12	13	14
Fischer			12	12	12	12	13	13	13
Karpov		7	8	8	9	10	11	12	13
Prodigies									
Reshevsky					7	7	8	9	10
Yanofsky						12	12	13	14
Pomar						10	11	12	13
Mecking						12	13	13	13
Contemporary Juniors									
Nigel Short (UK)	8	9	9	9	10	10	11	12	13
Gary Kasparov (USSR)						10	11	12	13
Joel Benjamin (USA)	10	11	11	11	11	11	12	13	
Junior World Champions									
Miles (UK)—1974				13	13	13	14	14	15
Diesen (USA)—1976								17	18

How to improve

1 Read chess books
2 Play against different people
3 Play against better opposition
4 Learn from your mistakes.

2400	2450	2500	2550	2600	2650	2700	2750	2800
					21			
	24	26	29	32				
			20	21		30	46	
17		18		20		24	32	
15		19		25		35	39	
19	20	22	24	27	34			
14	14	15	19	20	22	27	30	
15		16		18		28		
14		14		15		20		28
15		17		20		23	25	
19		23		24				
14		22						
19		28						
14		15		21				
18			20	21				
19	20